Guided By Grace

The Power of Surrendering to the Universe

Copyright© 2024 by Harsharan Gill-Kent

ISBN: 9798326445063

All Rights Reserved. No part of this book may be reproduced or transmitted in any form or by any means, electronic or mechanical, including photocopying, recording or by any information storage and retrieval system, without permission in writing from the copyright owner.

Dedicated to my beloved daughter Ashilda,

May this book guide you as you grow, teaching you the profound strength found in surrender. It is my hope that you discover, as you journey through life, that letting go and trusting the universe opens the heart to the deepest forms of love and wisdom. This is my gift to you—a map to finding grace under any circumstances.

CONTENTS

Preface 1

Chapter 1: Understanding Surrender 5

Chapter 2: Signs and Synchronicities 83

Chapter 3: Angels and Their Role in Our Lives . 101

Chapter 4: Letting Go Of Control 146

Chapter 5: Trusting the Journey 184

Chapter 6: Transformation Through Surrender . 202

Chapter 7 Living In Grace 223

Chapter 8 – Moving Forward in Faith 237

Preface

If someone had told me years ago that there would come a day when I'd see my greatest trials—not as curses, but as my most sacred teachers—I would have laughed, or more likely, cried in disbelief. Back then, I stood on the brink of what I perceived as the void, my business teetering on the edge of financial ruin, my personal savings a memory eroded by a relentless tide of bills and obligations. Money, that all-too-human measure of security and success, had slipped through my fingers, leaving me with nothing but a heavy heart and a troubled mind.

Yet, it was in this crucible of despair that an unexpected transformation began. Stripped of the material comforts and the illusory control I thought I had over my life; I was forced to confront my reality with a raw, unvarnished honesty. The journey from there to where I stand now was neither straight nor easy. I would describe it as walking through valleys shadowed by challenges and climbing up the peeks where the light seemed temporary. With every step, I felt myself letting go a bit more, giving in to a greater force – something divine that I had always felt but never embraced. This book is born from that journey. It is my heartfelt attempt to share not just the struggles and triumphs of my own path, but the profound wisdom that can only be found in the deepest of falls and the highest of climbs. It is a narrative of losing everything, only to find what truly matters, a story not of defeat, but of transformation and awakening.

The financial catastrophe that befell our business, and with that came chaos to my personal life, and this was my first true teacher. In the face of mounting debts and dwindling prospects, I experienced first-hand the futility of clinging to material solutions for spiritual problems. No amount of money could have saved me because what needed saving was not my bank account, but my soul. It took hitting rock bottom for me to realise that surrender was not a sign of weakness, but the most profound strength I could muster—the strength to let go of my ego, my plans, and my expectations, and to trust in the universe's plan for me.

Amidst this came up health issue which further stripped away any leftover illusions of control I had. When I was confronted by own mortality, I learned that true healing comes not from the external—be it medicine or money—but from an inner wellspring of faith and surrender. In my weakest moments, I discovered a pool of grace within, a divine support that carried me through when all else seemed lost.

This preface, and the pages that follow, are an invitation to you, to walk with me on this journey of surrender. It is my hope that by sharing my story, you might see reflections of your own struggles and aspirations and find comfort in the knowledge that you are not alone. We are all, in our own ways, navigating the tumultuous seas of life, seeking safe harbour, and meaning in the midst of our trials.

"Surrender" might feel like a surrender to the whims of fate or a passive acceptance of defeat. Yet, as you will see in these pages, it is anything but. Surrender is the active engagement of the soul with the divine, a conscious choice to trust in the guidance of higher forces, and an open-hearted acceptance of whatever comes our way, knowing that it comes with a purpose, a lesson, and a blessing.

This book is for anyone who's ever felt overwhelmed by the struggles of life, who's been through dark times and wondered if they'd ever see light again. It is for those who have felt the heavy burden of the world, who have wrestled with feelings of failure, loss, and despair, yet still cling to a sliver of hope. It is for anyone looking for moments of grace in the toughest times and longing to connect with something greater—a presence that speaks of a love so vast and deep it carries us through our darkest moments. This is a celebration of faith- not the loud, clanging kind, but the soft, steadfast kind that nurtures hope in the most barren places and believes through the coldest seasons. It honours the resilience of the human spirit, our incredible ability to rise from the ashes of our trials, reborn stronger, purer, and profoundly beautiful.

It acknowledges the boundless compassion of the universe, a force that guides us, supports us, and loves us unconditionally, even when we stray, even when we falter. This book is a bridge between the heart of the cosmos and the soul of the individual, a reminder that we are never truly alone, that we are forever held in the arms of a loving universe, guided by grace even when we are unaware.

As you turn these pages, I want you to open your heart to the possibility of transformation, to the miracles that await when we surrender with faith, and to the guidance that comes when we are most in need. Surrender here is not passive resignation but an active embrace of the universe's wisdom, a willing partnership with the divine in co-creating our destiny. It is an act of profound courage, a declaration of trust in the unseen, an open-hearted yes to the journey of becoming who we are meant to be.

Welcome to a journey of discovery, healing, and awakening. This journey is not just about finding answers but about learning to live the questions, to dance in the space between knowing and not knowing, and to find peace in the mystery. It is about seeing the divine in the mundane, the miraculous in the everyday, and understanding that every moment, no matter how small, has a possibility of grace.

Chapter 1: Understanding Surrender

Imagine you are holding onto a rope very tightly, and your hands are starting to hurt, and this rope represents trying to control everything in life—our plans, our dreams, even the things we can't really control. It is natural to hold on; it gives us a sense of security, a belief that if we just grip tightly enough, we can ensure everything goes exactly as we want. But this grip comes at a cost because our hands hurt, and our spirits tire from the constant tension and the fear of letting go.

Surrendering is like finally opening your hands and letting the rope fall and it doesn't mean you have lost or given up; It is about realising that some things are beyond our control, and that's perfectly okay. It is acknowledging that holding on so tightly was only causing more pain and that true peace comes from trusting enough to let go. The understanding that the universe has its rhythms and flows, its own way of balancing things out is what surrendering is. It is about trusting that things will work out as they are supposed to, even if it is not exactly how we imagined or envisioned.

This trust is not blind because it is built on a deep sense of connection with the world around us, a belief that there is something greater than us at play—a plan that is bigger and better than anything we could exactly map out. But embracing this is not always easy, especially in a society that values control and certainty above everything else. We are conditioned to believe that knowing where we are headed at every moment is the definition of success. But there is an immense beauty and freedom in becoming aware of that need for control. When we let go, we might fear that we will fall into chaos or lose our way. Yet, what actually unfolds is quite miraculous. We discover a new kind of order in our lives, an order that is not rigidly imposed upon us but naturally emerges. We find ourselves on a path that feels right, not because It is where we thought we should be, but because It is where we are meant to be.

This path of surrender doesn't lead us away from our dreams or desires; instead, it guides us towards them in a way that is more aligned with our true selves. It opens us up to new opportunities, ones we might never have considered had we stayed rigidly fixed on our initial course. It teaches us to be flexible, to adapt, and to find joy in the unexpected. Most importantly, it brings us into alignment with the universe's rhythms, allowing us to move with life's ebbs and flows rather than against them. This alignment doesn't just bring peace; it brings a sense of being deeply rooted in the truth of our existence, supported by the vast, intricate web of life that connects us all.

Surrender, then, is not just about letting go; It is about opening up to a richer, more meaningful way of living. It is about trusting that the universe, or whatever higher power you believe in, holds a wisdom far greater than our own. It is a journey from the tight grip of control to the open hands of grace, a journey that invites us to trust, to hope, and to find our place in the grand, unfolding tapestry of life.

Letting go and trusting the flow of life is not an invitation to passivity or inaction. Rather, It is an encouragement to engage with life more authentically, accepting that we won't always have the roadmap or the answers. This stance doesn't mean we stop making decisions or cease to strive towards our goals. Instead, it invites us to act with a sense of peace, knowing that our efforts are part of a larger tapestry, woven with threads we may not fully understand yet. It is like setting sail on the ocean with a compass rather than a map; we know the direction we want to go, but we remain open to the winds and currents that may take us on a different path than we planned. It is acknowledging, "I'm going to do my best, with the skills and knowledge I have, but I also recognise that I'm part of something bigger. I trust in that larger process, even when it leads me into the unknown."

Let's be clear, surrender is not giving up. To give up is to shut down, to reject possibilities before they have the chance to unfold, to harden ourselves against the potential for growth and change. Surrender, in contrast, is an act of opening. It is a conscious decision to remain receptive to the myriad possibilities' life offers, to say yes to the opportunities for growth and transformation. Choosing to trust in the face of uncertainty requires immense bravery and strength. It means acknowledging our fears and doubts, not as barriers, but as part of the human experience. To surrender is to lean into these feelings with faith, believing in a wisdom greater than our own, especially when the path forward is obscured by challenges. It is a powerful act of faith to stand in the midst of life's storms and choose to believe that there is a reason, a purpose, and a guiding hand behind it all.

The journey of surrender, while deeply transformative, unfolds within the most intimate spaces of our being. It is within these hidden chambers of the soul that true growth germinates, far from the glare of external achievements and societal accolades. This growth is subtle, often silent, nurtured by our openness to life's lessons, regardless of their guise. Each experience, whether cloaked in joy or shrouded in adversity, carries with it a kernel of wisdom, a lesson aimed not at our immediate gratification but at our profound evolution. This process of internal transformation is akin to the alchemy of the soul, where the raw ore of our experiences is transmuted into gold— into qualities of wisdom, compassion, and understanding that define the essence of who we are.

We are invariably met with moments that test the very limits of our capacity to trust and surrender as we navigate our life. When the ground beneath us seems to shift with each step, when shadows lengthen and the light dims, the call to surrender can feel like an echo in a void, distant and detached from our immediate reality. In these times, when every turn brings another challenge and every effort seems to unravel, the notion of surrender can appear counterintuitive, even impossible. How does one surrender when every fibre of being is geared towards resistance, towards fighting back against the tide? The answer does not lie in the denial of our struggles but in the acceptance of them as integral parts of our journey. Surrendering in difficult moments does not mean giving up the fight or diminishing the validity of our pain. It is rather about acknowledging our situation with honesty and bravery and choosing to trust in a greater process. It involves recognising that the universe is not working against us, but for us, in ways that our current perspective may not fully comprehend. It is about understanding that surrendering is not a passive act but a dynamic engagement with life, a willingness to ride the waves of uncertainty with faith that we will be carried to where we need to be.

This concept of surrender, especially in the face of adversity, is not just about weathering storms but about learning to see the lessons and opportunities that these storms bring. It is about finding peace amidst chaos, not by escaping the turmoil but by delving deeper into it, with the trust that there is light on the other side. Surrender, in this context, becomes a powerful act of courage, an affirmation of our faith in life's benevolence, even when it seems most elusive.

As we navigate through the complexities of surrender, we begin to see it not as a singular act but as a continuous process, a thread that weaves through the fabric of our daily lives. It is in the small moments as much as the monumental ones that we are invited to let go, to trust, and to open ourselves to the guidance that surrounds us. This ongoing engagement with surrender enriches our lives, infusing our actions with meaning and our path with clarity. It transforms surrender from a concept to be understood into a practice to be lived—a practice that, step by step, guides us closer to our true selves and to a deeper, more harmonious connection with the universe. In embracing surrender, we embrace the full spectrum of our human experience, trusting that each step, each challenge, and each moment of letting go is a step closer to our ultimate becoming.

Navigating the journey of surrender brings us into intimate contact with the very essence of life's ebb and flow. This path illuminates the truth that real growth and understanding burgeon not from the external accolades we accumulate, but from the quiet, steadfast unfolding within the depths of our being. It is a process that does not differentiate between moments of triumph and times of trial as vehicles for our evolution. Each experience, dressed in its unique garb of circumstance, carries with it the seeds of wisdom, beckoning us to cultivate a deeper, more nuanced comprehension of our existence. This inward journey transforms us, not by altering our outer world, but by reshaping our inner landscape, nurturing within us a wellspring of compassion, resilience, and insight.

The alchemy of transformation that occurs within these internal sanctuaries often finds its catalyst in the crucible of challenge. Difficult moments, those stretches of time when everything seems to be going wrong, are especially potent teachers on the path of surrender. The question then arises: How does one surrender when beset by a relentless storm of adversities, when each day seems to add weight to an already unbearable burden?

Surrendering in the face of such relentless challenges requires us to redefine our understanding of surrender itself. It is not about resignation or a passive acceptance of hardship. Rather, It is an active choice to trust in the midst of turmoil, to open our hearts to the lessons hidden within the pain, and to believe in the possibility of growth and renewal even when it seems most distant. It is about acknowledging our limitations and the reality of our situation while still maintaining hope, not in a specific outcome, but in the journey itself and in our capacity to endure, learn, and ultimately transcend our current circumstances.

This embrace of surrender does not negate the pain or difficulty of our trials. It does, however, offer a different lens through which to view them—one that recognise s each obstacle as an opportunity to deepen our understanding of ourselves and our place in the universe. In doing so, we begin to see that even in the darkest moments, there are glimmers of light, subtle indicators of the universe's support and guidance. Learning to recognise these signs amid adversity is a crucial aspect of the surrender process. It requires a sensitivity to the nuanced whispers of life, a readiness to perceive and accept guidance in its many forms.

As we learn to navigate surrender, not just as a concept but as a lived reality, we discover the profound trust required to let go and allow ourselves to be led by the unseen forces that guide our existence. This trust is not a blind leap into the abyss but a step into the light of greater awareness, armed with the knowledge that there is a harmony and order to the universe that, when aligned with, brings peace, clarity, and a deeper connection to all that is. Embracing this surrender transforms our relationship with life itself, turning what might have been a struggle for dominance into a dance with the divine, a partnership with the profound rhythms of existence.

In cultivating this trust and openness, we find that surrender becomes not just a strategy for navigating the difficult times, but a cornerstone of a life lived in deeper harmony with the world. It becomes a source of strength, a wellspring of grace that nourishes us, and a beacon guiding us toward our truest selves and the fulfilment of our highest potential.

In the heart of surrender lies the seed of transformation, a promise that even the most tumultuous times can be the soil from which new strength and understanding grow. This evolution of self is not just about acknowledging the silver linings in dark clouds but about weaving a tapestry where every thread, dark or bright, contributes to the beauty of the whole. The fabric of our lives becomes richer and more textured as we learn to embrace each moment with openness and trust, recognising the potential for growth and enlightenment within every experience.

The art of surrender asks us to lean into trust with all our being, to place our faith in the journey even when the destination is obscured by the fog of uncertainty. It invites us to listen more deeply to the whispers of the universe, to find solace in the knowledge that we are being guided, even when we feel most lost. This profound trust is not cultivated overnight; it grows from countless moments of choosing to believe in the goodness and purpose of the unfolding path, of recognising that each step, no matter how difficult, is moving us toward a deeper understanding of who we are and what we are capable of.

Incorporating surrender into our daily lives, especially during times of difficulty, begins with small, intentional acts of letting go. It might be as simple as taking a deep breath when we feel the impulse to control or fix a situation, reminding ourselves that we are part of a larger narrative. It might involve stepping back to view our challenges from a broader perspective, seeking the lessons they offer rather than fixating on the obstacles they present. Over time, these practices deepen our capacity for surrender, transforming it from an abstract concept into a tangible, lived experience. This lived experience of surrender becomes a powerful force in our lives, one that can transform fear into courage, confusion into clarity, and isolation into connection. As we grow in our ability to surrender, we discover a paradoxical truth: in letting go, we find a greater sense of control—not over the external world, but over our internal landscape. We learn to navigate life's storms with a steadier hand, guided by the light of our own inner compass, which points us toward peace, purpose, and a profound sense of belonging to something greater than ourselves.

Surrender, therefore, is not just a practice for the hard times; it is a way of being, a lens through which we can view every aspect of our lives. It teaches us to live with open hands and hearts, to embrace the journey of life with all its twists and turns, knowing that each moment is a step on the path to becoming our most authentic selves. It is a journey that invites us to let go of the illusion of control and to embrace the beauty of becoming, to trust deeply in the process of life, and to find within ourselves the courage to face each day with hope and openness.

As we delve deeper into the essence of surrender, recognising it as a powerful affirmation of our inner strength and resilience, we find ourselves at the cusp of a broader exploration. This understanding—that surrender is an active choice to live in harmony with the universe, to align with the ebb and flow of existence, and to welcome the grace that threads through our lives—serves as a bridge to the vast landscapes of history and culture. Here, surrender transcends the personal and touches the universal, revealing itself not merely as a practice but as a profound celebration of life. It becomes a dance with the divine, an invitation to discover the boundless possibilities that emerge when we release our grip and trust the path laid before us.

This seamless transition leads us into the rich tapestry of historical and cultural perspectives on surrender. As we turn our gaze to the diverse ways in which cultures and spiritual traditions around the world have embraced and interpreted the act of surrendering to a higher power or the flow of life, we embark on a journey through time and thought. This exploration is not only about understanding surrender as a concept but experiencing it as a universal human theme, reflecting the myriad ways in which people across ages and civilizations have sought to connect with something greater than themselves. Through this lens, surrender reveals itself as a timeless and transcendent principle, illuminating the shared human quest for meaning, connection, and the divine.

Historical and Cultural Perspectives

Embarking on a journey through the historical and cultural perspectives of surrender offers us a unique lens through which to view this profound concept. Across the vast tapestry of human civilization, cultures and spiritual traditions have grappled with the idea of surrendering to forces greater than themselves. Understanding these diverse interpretations not only deepens our comprehension but also illuminates the universal significance of surrender as a fundamental aspect of the human experience.

Surrender, in its essence, transcends the boundaries of time and place, emerging as a recurring theme that resonates with the core of our being. It is a concept that has guided societies through tumultuous times, offering solace and wisdom to those seeking direction and meaning. By exploring how different cultures and spiritual paths have embraced surrender, we uncover a rich mosaic of beliefs and practices that reveal the many facets of this complex theme.

This exploration is not merely academic; It is a journey that connects us with the shared struggles and aspirations of humanity. Through the lens of history and culture, we see how the act of surrender has been a gateway to understanding the mysteries of existence, a way to align with the divine, and a path to achieving a deeper sense of peace and fulfilment. Each tradition provides its own unique insights and practices, yet all point towards a common truth: that surrendering to something greater than ourselves is a powerful act of faith and courage.

As we delve into the historical and cultural perspectives on surrender, we invite readers to approach with an open mind and heart. This exploration offers an opportunity to appreciate the depth and breadth of human wisdom on surrender, enriching our own understanding and potentially transforming our approach to life's challenges. By recognising the universal threads that bind these diverse interpretations together, we come to see surrender not as a sign of weakness, but as a testament to the strength and resilience of the human spirit.

In this way, surrender becomes a profound celebration of life itself, inviting us to discover the endless possibilities that arise when we let go and trust in the journey. Through the stories, teachings, and practices of cultures around the world, we are reminded of the transformative power of surrender, and how it continues to inspire and guide us across the ages.

Embarking on a journey back to the cradle of civilization, we delve deep into the heart of ancient wisdom, traversing the sands of Egypt, walking the storied streets of Greece and Rome, and finally, venturing eastward into the rich spiritual tapestries of Hinduism and Buddhism. This panoramic voyage across time and philosophy uncovers the multifaceted interpretations of surrender, fate, and divine will, shedding light on the profound ways our ancestors engaged with these eternal truths.

Ancient Egypt: The Divine Order of Ma'at

In the sun-baked lands of Ancient Egypt, the concept of Ma'at reigned supreme, forming the bedrock of the society's understanding of the world. More than just an abstract idea, Ma'at was the very fabric of existence, representing truth, balance, order, harmony, law, morality, and justice. Envisioned as a goddess, Ma'at was the cosmic force that maintained the universe, ensuring the sun rose each day and the Nile flooded in its season, bringing life to the land.

The Egyptians viewed surrender to Ma'at not as a mere philosophical stance but as an essential way of life. It was believed that the stability of the cosmos itself depended on the alignment of human actions with this divine order. This active surrender was embodied in every aspect of Egyptian life, from the grandeur of the pharaohs' decrees to the daily rituals of the common people. Pharaohs, seen as the earthly representatives of Ma'at, were charged with the immense duty of upholding this cosmic balance, a task that required them to rule with justice and wisdom.

For the average Egyptian, surrendering to Ma'at meant living in accordance with principles of truth and harmony, both in their relationships with others and in their personal moral conduct. The societal norms, legal systems, and even the art and architecture of Egypt were all designed to reflect and reinforce Ma'at's principles, creating a society deeply intertwined with the rhythms of the natural world and the expectations of the divine.

Rituals played a significant role in this collective surrender to the divine order. Through offerings, prayers, and ceremonies, the Egyptians sought to appease the gods and ensure their favor, believing that such acts of devotion were crucial for the maintenance of Ma'at. Even in death, the ancient Egyptians' beliefs in Ma'at persisted, as seen in the weighing of the heart ceremony depicted in the Book of the Dead. Here, the deceased's heart was weighed against the feather of Ma'at, symbolizing truth and purity. A heart balanced with the feather ensured a favourable judgment and a peaceful afterlife, further emphasizing the paramount importance of living a life aligned with Ma'at.

Through the lens of Ma'at, we gain insight into the ancient Egyptians' profound understanding of surrender as an active engagement with the divine, a principle that guided them through the mysteries of life and death. This ancient wisdom reminds us that true balance and harmony are achieved not through the pursuit of personal desires but through the alignment of our actions with the universal order, a lesson as relevant today as it was thousands of years ago.

The ethos of Ma'at in Ancient Egypt was not confined to religious or philosophical realms but permeated every aspect of daily life, from the grand scale of constructing pyramids and temples designed to stand as eternal testaments to balance and symmetry, to the meticulous care with which scribes and artisans executed their crafts. This holistic integration of Ma'at into the fabric of Egyptian society illustrates a profound form of surrender, where every action, word, and thought was an opportunity to contribute to the harmony of the cosmos.

The influence of Ma'at extended into the administration of justice and governance. Courts and legal decisions sought to reflect Ma'at's principles, with fairness and truth serving as the cornerstones of the legal process. This was not merely a matter of law but a sacred duty; judges and officials were seen as instruments of Ma'at, ensuring that her divine order was mirrored in the human realm. Such was the depth of commitment to these principles that historical records and inscriptions often boast of rulers' adherence to Ma'at as their paramount achievement.

Moreover, the concept of Ma'at deeply influenced Egyptian artistic expression and architectural design. Temples, tombs, and monuments were constructed with an eye toward celestial alignments and proportions that reflected cosmic balance. Artistic depictions of Ma'at, often showing her with an ostrich feather, symbolized the lightness and purity that Egyptians aspired to in their own hearts. Through these artistic and architectural endeavours, the Egyptians sought to create a microcosm of the cosmos, a physical manifestation of the divine order on Earth.

The annual flooding of the Nile, essential for agriculture and survival, was also seen through the lens of Ma'at. This natural phenomenon was interpreted as a divine blessing, a manifestation of Ma'at's sustaining harmony. The predictability and bounty of the floodwaters reaffirmed the Egyptians' belief in a cosmos governed by a just and orderly principle, encouraging a societal attitude of gratitude and reverence towards the natural world.

Even in the realm of personal ethics and morality, Ma'at played a pivotal role. The concept of the "42 Negative Confessions" or "Declarations of Innocence" in the Book of the Dead exemplifies this, where the deceased proclaims their adherence to Ma'at's principles by denying any breach of her laws. These confessions cover a wide range of moral and ethical principles, from the prohibition of theft and lying to the imperative of respect for one's parents and neighbours. Through these declarations, the individual aligns themselves with the cosmic order, aspiring to a state of purity and balance that mirrors Ma'at.

In exploring the ancient Egyptian concept of Ma'at, we encounter a civilization that viewed surrender not as subjugation but as a profound engagement with the divine. This engagement was active and intentional, permeating every layer of society and influencing every aspect of individual life. The Egyptians' dedication to living in accordance with Ma'at teaches us the power of aligning our actions with universal principles of truth, balance, and harmony. It is a testament to the belief that individual and collective well-being is deeply connected to the cosmic order, a belief that continues to inspire and challenge us to find harmony in our own lives.

Ancient Greece and Rome: Fate and the Will of the Gods

As we transition from the harmonious banks of the Nile to the storied realms of Ancient Greece and Rome, we find a shift in how civilizations perceived the concepts of surrender, fate, and divine will. The journey from Ma'at's orderly cosmos leads us into the heart of Mediterranean antiquity, where the capricious whims of gods and the inexorable march of fate shaped the lives of mortals.

In Ancient Greece, the concept of fate, or Moira, held a grip as tight as the Olympian gods themselves. The Greeks saw their lives as threads woven by the Fates, three sisters who determined the lifespan and destiny of each individual. This understanding permeated Greek mythology, where tales of heroes and mortals alike illustrated the futility of attempting to outmanoeuvre one's destined path. Yet, it was this very struggle against fate that often defined Greek heroism, highlighting a complex interplay between human agency and divine decree.

Oracle sites like Delphi served as nexus points between the mortal and divine, where individuals and states sought guidance from the gods through cryptic prophecies. Surrendering to the will of the gods, as revealed through oracles and omens, was a nuanced affair; it required interpretation, faith, and often, a willingness to engage in actions that might seem at odds with one's desires or understanding. This dance with fate and divine will underscored the Greek belief in the importance of striving for arete, or excellence, within the bounds set by the gods.

The Romans, inheriting and adapting the Greek pantheon, emphasized the virtue of pietas, or piety, which included a sense of duty not only to the gods but to family and state. This duty was a form of surrender to the will of the gods, manifesting in religious rituals, personal conduct, and the service to the Roman Republic, and later, the Empire. The Romans believed that their success and expansion were indications of their favour with the gods, with the state's fortunes rising or falling based on their collective adherence to divine will.

Roman literature and philosophy often grappled with the tension between fatum (fate) and the exercise of human free will. Stoicism, a school of philosophy that flourished in the Greco-Roman world, offered a way to navigate this tension. Stoics advocated for an acceptance of fate as part of the natural order, emphasizing that true freedom and tranquillity come from aligning one's desires and actions with the course of nature, which was ultimately governed by divine reason.

As we reflect on the ancient Greek and Roman worlds, we see a landscape rich with tales of gods and humans, heroes and commoners, all intertwined in the dance of fate and free will. Their stories remind us that the quest to understand our place in the universe and to surrender to forces beyond our control is a timeless endeavour, echoing across the ages. Through their struggles and triumphs, we learn that surrendering to the divine will or the dictates of fate does not negate human agency but rather frames it within a broader cosmic narrative, offering insights into courage, virtue, and the pursuit of meaning in a world governed by powers beyond mortal ken.

In the heart of Ancient Greece, the interplay between human ambition and divine prerogative unfolds across epic tales and tragedies, where heroes like Achilles and Odysseus navigate the turbulent waters of fate and free will. These narratives are not mere stories but reflections of a deeply held belief in the power and capriciousness of the gods. The Greek understanding of surrender was complex, embodying a recognition of the limits of human control against the backdrop of divine omnipotence. Heroes striving against their fates, as foretold by oracles and auguries, become emblematic of the human condition, revealing a profound engagement with the notion of surrender as an existential struggle.

This engagement is vividly illustrated in the Oracle of Delphi, where kings and warriors sought the counsel of the Pythia, a priestess believed to channel the god Apollo's wisdom. The cryptic pronouncements from Delphi required not just passive acceptance but a deep contemplation of one's path, a surrender to the divine will that was active and participatory. The Greeks' quest for knowledge and understanding of the gods' will was a testament to their desire to coexist with the forces that shaped their lives, embodying a form of surrender that was both a concession to and an engagement with the divine.

Transitioning to Ancient Rome, the spiritual landscape morphs, yet the thread of fate and divine will continues to weave through the fabric of Roman society. Romans embraced a pantheon of gods, carrying forward and reshaping the Greek gods in their own image. The Roman virtue of pietas, extending beyond mere religious devotion to encompass a duty to family and the state, underscored the societal importance of surrendering personal desires to the collective needs and the decrees of fate and the gods. This sense of duty was a cornerstone of Roman identity, reflecting a broader cultural surrender to the structures and hierarchies believed to be sanctioned by the divine.

The Stoic philosophy, which found fertile ground in the Roman intellectual terrain, provided a framework for understanding and embracing fate. Stoicism taught that while we cannot control external events, we can control our reactions to them, advocating for an inner surrender to the logic of the cosmos, which was seen as rational and providential. This surrender was not passive but a dynamic acceptance that freed individuals from the turmoil of desire and aversion. Marcus Aurelius, a Stoic philosopher, and Roman Emperor, epitomizes this approach, his Meditations serving as a timeless guide to finding peace and purpose in a world governed by forces beyond our control.

The ancient Greeks and Romans, through their myths, philosophies, and daily practices, contributed enduring insights into the nature of surrender. Their legacy teaches us that surrender to fate or the divine will is not about relinquishing our agency but about recognising and embracing our place within a larger order. This understanding invites us to reflect on our own lives, considering how we might navigate our destinies with a blend of humility, courage, and wisdom. Through the lens of these ancient civilizations, we see that the act of surrender, far from signalling defeat, is a profound affirmation of life's richness and the intricate dance between human aspirations and the divine tapestry of the universe.

Sikhism: The Path of Surrender through Divine Love and Will

In the spiritual tapestry of the world, Sikhism emerges as a vibrant thread, weaving a distinct narrative around the concept of surrender. Founded in the 15th century in the Punjab region of South Asia by Guru Nanak Dev Ji, Sikhism introduces a unique blend of devotion, community, and the pursuit of justice, cantered on the principle of surrender to the Divine Will, or Hukam.

Sikhism teaches that the ultimate reality is Waheguru, the Eternal Guru, and that understanding and accepting Hukam is key to aligning with divine will. Hukam, which can be understood as the divine order or command, is not merely about fatalism or passivity but involves an active, conscious surrender. This surrender is rooted in love and devotion for the Divine, encapsulated in the practice of Bhakti.

Guru Nanak, the first of the ten Sikh Gurus, laid the foundation for this path of surrender. His teachings emphasize the importance of recognising one's own will as subordinate to the divine will. By understanding and accepting Hukam, one can live a life of contentment, peace, and harmony, transcending the ego and the illusions that bind the soul to the cycle of birth and rebirth.

This concept of surrender is further elaborated through the Sikh practice of Naam Simran, the meditation and chanting of the Divine Name. This practice is a form of surrender, a tool to cleanse the mind and soul, bringing the practitioner closer to the Divine and fostering a deep, personal connection with Waheguru. It is through this loving remembrance that Sikhs cultivate an awareness of God's presence in all aspects of life, seeing the Divine hand in the unfolding of each moment.

The Sikh Gurus also emphasized the importance of Seva, or selfless service, as a means of surrendering the ego. Serving others without expectation of reward or recognition is seen as serving God Himself, as all are considered part of the same divine creation. This service is a practical manifestation of surrender, embodying the Sikh ideal of living in the world but not being of it, engaging in society's welfare while keeping the consciousness attuned to the Divine.

The concept of surrender in Sikhism is thus multifaceted, involving the surrender of the ego, the acceptance of God's will, and the cultivation of love and devotion through remembrance and service. The ultimate aim is to merge the individual soul with the Supreme Soul, achieving a state of eternal bliss and liberation.

Sikhism's perspective enriches our exploration of surrender, showcasing it as an act of profound faith and love. It teaches us that surrender is not a defeat but a victory of the spirit, a harmonious alignment with the Divine that brings deep peace and fulfilment. Through the teachings of the Gurus, enshrined in the Guru Granth Sahib, Sikhism offers a path that blends devotion, action, and ethical living into a holistic practice of surrender, guiding followers toward a life of compassion, righteousness, and divine communion.

Sikhism, emerging in the 15th century in the region of Punjab, India, introduces a unique perspective on surrender through its foundational teachings and practices. Founded by Guru Nanak Dev Ji, and further shaped by nine successive Gurus, Sikhism emphasizes a direct connection with the divine, without the need for rituals or intermediaries. At the heart of Sikh philosophy lies the principle of surrendering to the Will of God, or Waheguru, a concept deeply embedded in the daily lives and spiritual practices of Sikhs.

Embracing Hukam: Understanding Divine Will

Central to the Sikh view of surrender is the concept of Hukam, or divine order. Unlike passive resignation, understanding and accepting Hukam involves recognising the omnipresence and omnipotence of Waheguru in every aspect of life. Sikhs believe that everything in the universe operates under God's command, and human beings achieve true peace and fulfilment by aligning their will with the divine will. This alignment is not seen as a loss of freedom but as the ultimate liberation from the ego and the cycles of birth and rebirth.

Guru Nanak Dev Ji's teachings emphasize the importance of living in harmony with Hukam, urging followers to cultivate an attitude of acceptance and gratitude, regardless of life's circumstances. This philosophy encourages Sikhs to view life's joys and challenges as part of a larger, divine plan, beyond human understanding and control.

Simran and Seva: Active Surrender through Devotion and Service

Sikhism advocates for an active form of surrender, primarily through the practices of Simran (remembrance of God's name) and Seva (selfless service). Simran involves constant meditation on the name and nature of God, fostering a deep, personal connection with the divine. This practice is a form of surrender, as it requires the individual to focus their thoughts and energies on Waheguru, transcending personal desires and the distractions of the material world.

Seva, or selfless service, is another pillar of Sikh practice that exemplifies active surrender. Sikhs are encouraged to serve humanity without any expectation of reward, seeing the divine in everyone. This act of service is a practical manifestation of surrendering the ego, as it shifts the focus from the self to the welfare of the community and the broader creation. Through Seva, Sikhs embody the values of compassion, humility, and equality, reflecting the divine order in their actions.

The Guru Granth Sahib: The Living Guru

The Guru Granth Sahib, Sikhism's holy scripture, serves as the eternal Guru and a guiding light for Sikhs worldwide. This sacred text contains the hymns and teachings of the Sikh Gurus, along with those of saints from various faiths, underscoring the universal nature of its wisdom. The Guru Granth Sahib emphasizes the unity of God, the equality of all beings, and the importance of living an honest, disciplined life dedicated to service and remembrance of God.

For Sikhs, surrender to the divine will is intricately linked to the teachings of the Guru Granth Sahib. Engaging with the scripture through daily reading and reflection helps Sikhs to internalize the concept of Hukam, guiding them toward a life of deeper spiritual fulfilment and harmony with the divine order.

In exploring Sikhism's approach to surrender, we uncover a path that combines devotion, service, and a profound acceptance of divine will. Sikh teachings offer a powerful perspective on how surrender can lead to spiritual liberation, peace, and a sense of unity with the divine and all creation. Through the principles of Hukam, Simran, and Seva, Sikhism presents a dynamic and active approach to surrender, one that enriches the individual and the community, aligning them with the cosmic order and the timeless flow of divine grace.

Hinduism: Surrender and Devotion in the Eternal Dharma

Hinduism, with its profound spiritual heritage, offers a rich tapestry of insights into the nature of surrender. Rooted in the ancient Vedas, this timeless tradition views surrender not merely as an act of devotion but as an essential pathway to liberation and union with the Divine. Central to Hindu philosophy is the concept of Bhakti, or devotional surrender, where the devotee offers their love and loyalty to God unconditionally, transcending the ego to merge with the divine essence.

Bhakti Yoga: The Path of Devotional Surrender
Bhakti Yoga, one of the paths to spiritual realisation in Hinduism, emphasizes surrender to God as the highest form of worship. This path is beautifully illustrated in the epic tale of the Bhagavad Gita, where Lord Krishna imparts spiritual wisdom to the warrior prince Arjuna. Faced with the moral dilemma of battling his own kin, Arjuna is counselled by Krishna to perform his duty (dharma) as an act of surrender to the

divine will, without attachment to the results of his actions.

This teaching underscores the essence of Bhakti Yoga, where surrender involves a deep trust in the divine plan, even in the face of life's greatest challenges. Devotees engage in practices such as chanting, prayer, and rituals not as mere formalities but as expressions of their heartfelt devotion and surrender to God. Through Bhakti, the individual soul (Atman) seeks to reunite with the universal soul (Brahman), transcending the illusions of separation and ego.

Karma Yoga: Surrender through Selfless Action
Karma Yoga, another path outlined in the Bhagavad Gita, teaches surrender through selfless action. Here, surrender is understood as performing one's duties with excellence and dedication, without attachment to personal gain or outcomes. This practice encourages individuals to see their work and responsibilities as offerings to the divine, fostering a sense of humility and detachment from the fruits of their labour.

Karma Yoga promotes the idea that true fulfilment comes from serving others and contributing to the greater good, aligning one's actions with dharma, or cosmic law. This alignment requires surrendering personal desires and ambitions to the divine will, recognising that every action is part of a larger, divine orchestration.

Jnana Yoga: Surrender through Knowledge

Jnana Yoga, the path of knowledge and wisdom, involves surrendering the intellect and ego to attain spiritual enlightenment. This path challenges devotees to question the nature of reality, the self, and the universe, using discernment and meditation to pierce through the veil of ignorance (Avidya).

Surrender in Jnana Yoga is an inward journey, where the individual relinquishes their preconceived notions and false identities to realise their true, divine nature. This profound understanding leads to Moksha, or liberation from the cycle of birth and rebirth (Samsara), marking the ultimate surrender of the soul to the eternal truth of Brahman.

The Upanishads and Vedanta: Unifying Visions of Surrender

The teachings of the Upanishads and the Vedanta philosophy further elaborate on the concept of surrender. These texts, which form the philosophical foundation of Hinduism, explore the deep interconnectedness of the individual soul with the universal spirit. They teach that surrendering the ego and realising the oneness of Atman and Brahman is the key to achieving eternal bliss and liberation.

In these sacred writings, surrender is portrayed as the dissolution of the individual self into the boundless ocean of divine consciousness. Through devotion, selfless action, and the pursuit of wisdom, the devotee transcends the limitations of the material world, embracing the infinite and eternal nature of the divine.

Hinduism's multifaceted approach to surrender—through Bhakti, Karma, and Jnana Yoga, as well as its foundational texts—provides a comprehensive framework for understanding and practicing surrender. Each path offers unique insights into how surrendering to the divine leads to spiritual growth, harmony, and ultimate liberation, illustrating the diverse yet unified nature of Hindu spiritual practice.

Exploring the depth of Hinduism's approach to surrender, particularly through Bhakti Yoga, unveils a vibrant tapestry of devotion and spiritual longing that has inspired millions over centuries. Bhakti Yoga transcends mere ritualistic practices, inviting devotees into a heartfelt relationship with the divine, characterized by love, devotion, and a profound sense of surrender. This path illuminates the soul's journey towards union with the divine, emphasizing personal experience and emotional connection over intellectual understanding.

The Bhagavad Gita: Arjuna's Dilemma and Divine Surrender

The Bhagavad Gita, a cornerstone of Hindu philosophy, provides a compelling narrative framework for the exploration of surrender. On the battlefield of Kurukshetra, Prince Arjuna is torn between his duty as a warrior and his moral qualms about fighting his own kin. It is Lord Krishna's divine counsel that guides Arjuna, revealing the deeper spiritual truths of existence, duty, and devotion. Krishna's teachings emphasize that true surrender involves performing one's dharma with complete faith in the divine, relinquishing attachment to the outcomes.

This narrative encapsulates the essence of Bhakti Yoga, where surrender is not passive but an active engagement in one's duties, infused with love and devotion for God. Krishna encourages Arjuna to see his actions as offerings to the divine, fostering a detachment from egoistic desires and outcomes. This surrender to God's will is what ultimately leads to liberation and enlightenment, as Arjuna learns to act in the world with a spirit of selflessness and devotion.

The Role of Devotional Practices in Bhakti Yoga
In the path of Bhakti Yoga, devotional practices such as chanting (kirtan), prayer (puja), and meditation on the names and forms of God are vital expressions of surrender. These practices allow devotees to connect with the divine on a deeply personal level, cultivating an inner environment of devotion and surrender. Through the repetition of God's name, the devotee's mind is purified, and their heart is opened to receive divine grace. These practices serve not just as acts of worship but as means of dissolving the ego and fostering a profound union with the divine.

The emotional intensity and personal nature of Bhakti Yoga make it a path accessible to all, regardless of social status or intellectual prowess. It democratizes the spiritual quest, emphasizing the heart's purity over ritualistic precision or philosophical sophistication. This universality of Bhakti Yoga underscores the inclusive nature of Hinduism, where the divine is accessible to anyone who approaches with a sincere and devoted heart.

Surrender in the Lives of Bhakti Saints

The tradition of Bhakti Yoga is rich with stories of saints and mystics who embodied the essence of surrender in their lives. Figures such as Mirabai, a devotee of Krishna, and Kabir, a poet-saint who blended Hindu and Muslim spiritual insights, exemplify the transformative power of surrender. Their lives and poetry convey a deep, abiding love for the divine, transcending religious boundaries and societal norms. These saints exemplify how surrender to God leads to spiritual liberation, transcending the cycle of birth and rebirth through the power of devotion.

Their stories highlight the intimate, personal nature of the divine relationship sought in Bhakti Yoga, where God is not a distant, impersonal force but a beloved, with whom the devotee seeks union. This relationship is marked by a sweetness and intensity of emotion that can only arise from the complete surrender of the self to the divine will.

Integrating Surrender into Daily Life

Bhakti Yoga offers practical guidance for integrating surrender into everyday life. Devotees are encouraged to see every moment as an opportunity to practice devotion and surrender, whether through formal worship, acts of kindness, or the simple remembrance of God throughout the day. This constant awareness cultivates a living relationship with the divine, transforming mundane activities into expressions of love and surrender.

Bhakti Yoga's approach to surrender within Hinduism offers a profound path to spiritual realisation, emphasizing the power of love and devotion. Through the teachings of the Bhagavad Gita, the practices of chanting, prayer, and meditation, and the inspiring lives of Bhakti saints, devotees are guided towards a life of surrender, where every action is infused with devotion and every moment is an opportunity for spiritual union with the divine. This path illuminates the heart's capacity to transcend the ego and merge with the infinite, revealing the boundless possibilities of the soul's journey towards divine love.

Jewish Traditions of Surrender to God's Will in the Torah

After exploring the spiritual landscapes of Asian cultures, our journey leads us to the fertile crescent and beyond, where the Abrahamic religions—

Judaism, Christianity, and Islam—emerge. Here, in the ancient narratives and teachings of Judaism, we encounter a deep-rooted tradition of surrender to God's will, a theme that is both timeless and transformative.

At the heart of Jewish spiritual life is the covenant, a foundational concept that epitomizes surrender to God. This sacred agreement, initiated between God and Abraham, represents a mutual commitment: divine protection and blessing in exchange for unwavering faith and obedience. This moment, chronicled in the Torah, is not merely a historical or theological event but a profound act of surrender from Abraham, who accepts God's will with complete trust, even when the path ahead is veiled in uncertainty.

The covenant with Abraham sets a precedent for his descendants, becoming a cornerstone of Jewish identity and faith. It is a relationship that demands not just adherence to a set of laws but a heartfelt surrender to God's guidance, a theme that resonates through the generations. From Isaac's willingness to be bound on the altar, to Jacob's wrestle with the divine, to Joseph's resilience in Egypt, the narratives of the Patriarchs and Matriarchs are imbued with acts of faith and surrender, illustrating a deep engagement with the divine will.

This theme of surrender is further woven into the fabric of Jewish life through the observance of the commandments, or mitzvot. These are not seen merely as obligations or burdens but as opportunities to align one's life with the divine will, fostering a living relationship with God. Each commandment, whether it concerns ethics, ritual practice, or personal conduct, becomes a manifestation of surrender to God, an expression of trust and devotion that transcends the mundane aspects of daily life.

The covenant also carries a communal dimension of surrender, where the collective faith and obedience of the Jewish people contribute to the sustenance of their relationship with God. Central to this is the observance of celebrations, memorials, and rituals that define the rhythm of Jewish life, all of which revolve around the covenant's enduring legacy.

One such observance is Yom Kippur, the Day of Atonement, considered the holiest day in Judaism. It is a day dedicated to solemn introspection, prayer, and fasting, where individuals reflect on their actions over the past year, seeking forgiveness and committing to personal and communal improvement in the year ahead. Yom Kippur embodies the essence of surrender to God's will, as individuals and communities alike engage in a profound spiritual inventory, acknowledging their shortcomings and expressing a sincere desire to align more closely with divine expectations.

Equally significant is Passover, a joyous festival that commemorates the liberation of the Israelites from Egyptian bondage. It is a time of reflection on the themes of freedom, redemption, and the miraculous intervention of God in history. Through the retelling of the Exodus story, participants are reminded of their ancestors' trust in God's promise and the importance of maintaining faith even in times of great adversity.

These communal observances, from the reflective depth of Yom Kippur to the liberatory celebration of Passover, reinforce the covenant's significance, reminding each generation of their ancestral commitment to divine surrender. By participating in these rituals, the Jewish people not only commemorate historical events but also reaffirm their ongoing relationship with God, based on the foundational principles of faith, trust, and obedience laid down by the covenant.

In the midst of trials and tribulations, the covenant has served as a beacon of hope and resilience for the Jewish people. The history of Judaism is replete with moments of hardship and persecution, yet the covenantal promise has remained a source of strength, inspiring countless individuals to renew their faith and surrender to God's will, even in the face of adversity.

By delving into the covenant at the heart of Judaism, we gain insights into the profound and multifaceted nature of surrender. It is a concept that encompasses trust, obedience, and a deep-seated belief in the benevolence of the divine plan. Through this lens, the rich spiritual heritage of Judaism offers timeless lessons on the transformative power of surrender, inviting us to reflect on our own relationship with the divine and the ways in which we might live more fully in alignment with a higher will.

Torah and Commandments: The Path of Surrender

Central to Jewish life and spiritual practice is the Torah, alongside the myriad commandments it contains, which serve as a comprehensive guide for living in alignment with God's will. The observance of these mitzvot, which span ethical behaviours, ritual practices, and daily prayers, represents an active and conscious commitment to divine surrender. This dedication to obedience is not perceived as a burden but rather as an opportunity to sanctify everyday life and enhance one's connection with God.

Embedded within the Torah is the story of the Exodus, a narrative that remains a cornerstone of Jewish identity and faith. It recounts the journey of Moses and the Israelites from the depths of slavery in Egypt to their liberation and emergence as a nation under God's protection. This historical saga is not just a tale of physical freedom but also a profound lesson in spiritual surrender. It highlights the transformative power of faith and obedience, as the Israelites navigate the challenges of the wilderness, relying on God's guidance and providence.

The climax of this journey occurs at Mount Sinai, where the giving of the Torah to Moses and the Israelites marks a pivotal moment in their relationship with God. Here, the covenant is renewed, and the Israelites affirm their commitment to live according to God's laws. Their acceptance of the Torah signifies a collective act of surrender, not out of resignation but out of a deep sense of trust and reverence. It is a moment that encapsulates the essence of their identity as a people chosen to uphold a sacred bond with the divine.

This historical narrative and the ongoing practice of the mitzvot in Jewish life underscore the dynamic nature of surrender. It is an act that involves both the heart and the will, requiring individuals and communities to continually choose faithfulness to God's commandments. Through this process, life itself becomes an expression of devotion, each act of observance a reaffirmation of the covenant and a step closer to the divine.

In embracing the Torah and its commandments, Jews find not just a set of rules but a path to spiritual elevation, a way to infuse the divine into the mundane, transforming everyday actions into sacred deeds. This path of surrender, illuminated by the Torah, offers profound insights into the nature of faith, obedience, and the pursuit of a life lived in harmony with the divine will.

Prayer and Ritual: Expressions of Surrender

In the heart of Jewish spirituality, prayer emerges as a profound dialogue with the Divine, a daily practice where the soul's surrender to God is voiced. Among these prayers, the Shema stands as a testament to the depth of this surrender, with its profound declaration of God's unity and the call to love and serve Him with every facet of one's being. This prayer is not just a statement of faith; it is a commitment, a pledge to live every moment under the auspices of divine will.

This dedication extends beyond the personal realm into the communal through the observance of rituals and sacred times. The Sabbath, with its invitation to rest and reflect, acts as a weekly reminder of God's creation and providence, offering a space to celebrate the divine order. Jewish festivals, tracing the arc of historical and spiritual milestones, immerse the community in the rhythm of divine time, each observance a mosaic of remembrance, gratitude, and surrender. Life cycle events, from birth through to death, mark the individual's journey within this covenant, framing each life stage as an opportunity to recognise and affirm God's presence and plan.

Suffering and Trust: The Challenge of Surrender
The path of surrender within Judaism is not without its trials. The historical narrative of the Jewish people is punctuated by moments of profound suffering and displacement, each episode a crucible testing the strength and depth of their faith. Yet, it is through these periods of hardship that the essence of Jewish surrender is most vividly illuminated, revealing a trust in God that transcends the immediate pain and seeks

understanding in the broader context of divine justice and love.

The Book of Job stands as a poignant exploration of this theme, where righteousness and suffering intersect, challenging the faithful to maintain their trust in God's goodness despite the apparent absence of reason. Job's story is a meditation on the mystery of divine will, inviting believers to grapple with the complexity of faith when faced with inexplicable loss and pain. It underscores that surrender to God's will is not a passive acceptance but an active trust, a faith that engages with the divine even when the path is obscured.

A Holistic Approach to Faith

The intricate weave of Jewish tradition, with its rich fabric of history, law, prayer, and ritual, portrays surrender to God's will as a holistic way of life. It is a path that encompasses both the heights of joy and the depths of sorrow, offering a means to navigate the complexities of existence with grace and faith. In Judaism, surrender is not merely a concept but a lived experience, an ever-present dialogue between the individual, the community, and the Divine.

Through this enduring commitment to live according to divine guidance, Judaism presents a vibrant exploration of surrender. It is a faith tradition that speaks to the heart of what it means to be human, offering insights into the act of surrender as both a personal devotion and a communal covenant. In the reflection of its prayers, the rhythm of its rituals, and the resilience of its people, Judaism invites us all to contemplate the profound peace and purpose found in surrendering to something greater than ourselves.

Christianity: The Path of Trust and Surrender

In the mosaic of Abrahamic traditions, Christianity occupies a central place, weaving its own unique narrative around the concepts of surrender, faith, and trust in God. The Christian tradition, with its rich tapestry of biblical narratives, hymns, and theological discourse, offers profound insights into the nature of surrender to God's will. At the heart of this tradition is the life and teachings of Jesus Christ, who exemplifies the ultimate act of surrender and obedience to God.

The Life of Jesus: An Emblem of Surrender

The life of Jesus Christ, as recounted in the New Testament, embodies the essence of surrender to God. From His birth in a humble manger to His crucifixion and resurrection, Jesus' life is a testament to the power of divine surrender. His ministry, marked by teachings of love, compassion, and forgiveness, underscores a deep reliance on and trust in God's plan.

One of the most poignant examples of surrender in the Christian tradition is found in the Garden of Gethsemane, where Jesus, facing imminent arrest and crucifixion, prays to God, saying, "Not my will, but yours be done" (Luke 22:42). This moment encapsulates the depth of Jesus' surrender, showcasing His willingness to accept God's will, even in the face of suffering and death. It is a powerful illustration of faith and trust in God, serving as a model for Christians to follow in their own lives.

Biblical Narratives of Surrender

Beyond the life of Jesus, the Bible is replete with narratives that highlight the theme of surrender to God's will. The story of Abraham's willingness to sacrifice his son Isaac at God's command, only to be stopped at the last moment, is another profound example. This story, shared with Judaism, emphasizes obedience and faith in God's provision and promises.

Similarly, the narrative of Job, who remains faithful despite immense suffering and loss, challenges and deepens the understanding of surrender. Job's story prompts believers to trust in God's wisdom and justice, even when His plans are beyond human understanding. The New Testament letters, particularly those of Paul, further explore the theme of surrender through the lens of Christian faith. Paul's writings encourage believers to present themselves as "living sacrifices" to God (Romans 12:1), highlighting a life of surrender as an act of worship and devotion.

Christian Practices of Surrender

In Christian practice, surrender to God is expressed through prayer, worship, and the sacraments. Prayer, especially the Lord's Prayer, offers a model for surrender, with petitions like "Thy will be done" echoing Jesus' own surrender in Gethsemane. Worship services, hymns, and liturgical practices also provide spaces for Christians to collectively affirm their trust in God and their desire to align their lives with His will.

The sacraments, particularly baptism and the Eucharist, symbolize surrender to God's grace and the transformative power of the Holy Spirit. Through these rites, believers are invited to die to themselves and live for Christ, embodying the surrender of their own wills to the divine purpose.

Surrender in Christian Theology and Spirituality
Christian theology and spirituality further explore the implications of surrender for the believer's life. The concept of "dying to self" and being "born again" in Christ reflects the transformative aspect of surrender, where letting go of one's ego and desires leads to new life in the spirit. Mystics and theologians throughout Christian history, from Augustine to Teresa of Avila to Dietrich Bonhoeffer, have delved into the mysteries of surrender, offering insights into its role in deepening one's relationship with God and advancing on the spiritual path.

In the Christian understanding, surrender is not a one-time act but a continuous journey of faith and trust. It involves daily decisions to follow Christ, to take up one's cross, and to live in accordance with God's will. This journey is marked by challenges and sacrifices but also by profound joy and peace, as believers experience the presence and guidance of God in their lives.

Within the heart of Christianity lies a profound narrative of surrender, intricately interwoven into its sacred scriptures, enduring traditions, and daily practices. This narrative offers a rich exploration into the essence of living in profound trust and obedience to God. Central to this exploration is the life of Jesus Christ—His teachings, actions, and ultimate sacrifice—serving as the quintessential example of surrender to the divine will. The stories of biblical figures, coupled with the lived experiences of countless believers through history, collectively illustrate the transformative power of surrender, unveiling the profound truths about strength, freedom, and the human spirit.

Surrender in Christianity is not merely about relinquishing control but engaging in a deeper, more meaningful dialogue with the divine. It is about finding one's true purpose and peace in the alignment with God's will, a journey marked not by passivity but by active, loving trust. The life and teachings of Jesus Christ, together with the narratives of faith found throughout the Bible, reveal that true empowerment and liberation emerge from the act of yielding one's will to God, embracing faith and trust in His benevolent plan for all creation.

This dynamic of surrender invites believers into a participatory role in God's redemptive work, calling them to live out the values of grace, love, and hope in a tangible manner. It is through this act of surrender that Christians find themselves co-creators with God, contributing to the unfolding of divine grace in the world. By laying down their own desires and ambitions at the feet of the divine will, believers open themselves to a greater understanding of God's love and the mysteries of faith.

As Christians navigate the complexities of life, guided by the examples of surrender found in their sacred texts and tradition, they are continually reminded of the power of surrender to transform lives. It is a journey of constant growth, learning, and deepening of faith, where every act of trust and submission becomes a testament to the enduring hope and grace that define their spiritual path. Through surrender, the Christian faith offers not just a roadmap for spiritual enlightenment but a way to engage with the world that is reflective of God's love and compassion for humanity.

Islam: Embracing Divine Surrender in the Contemporary World

In the vast panorama of world religions, Islam stands prominently, embodying the essence of surrender in its very name. Derived from the Arabic root word 'aslama', which means to submit or surrender, Islam calls its followers to a life of complete submission to Allah's will. This central tenet of Islamic faith is beautifully encapsulated in the Quran, the holy book of Islam, which provides guidance on how to live a life that is in harmony with God's commands and creation.

The Quran: Guidance on Surrender to Allah

The Quran, revealed to Prophet Muhammad over 23 years, is considered the direct word of God by Muslims around the world. It serves not only as a spiritual guide but also as a comprehensive manual for living a life aligned with the divine will. Throughout its verses, the Quran emphasizes the importance of surrender to Allah, presenting it as the foundation of faith and the pathway to peace and salvation.

One of the key aspects of surrender in Islam is the concept of Tawhid, the Oneness of Allah. Tawhid is the acknowledgment that Allah is the sole creator, and ruler of the universe, and that there is no power or authority except that which He grants. This belief requires Muslims to place their trust wholly in Allah, recognising His wisdom and mercy in all affairs, both personal and universal.

Submission Through Worship and Obedience

Islamic practice offers tangible expressions of surrender through the Five Pillars of Islam, which outline the essential acts of worship required of every Muslim. These include the Shahada (declaration of faith), Salat (five daily prayers), Zakat (almsgiving), Sawm (fasting during Ramadan), and Hajj (pilgrimage to Mecca). Each of these practices serves as a reminder of the believer's commitment to submit to Allah's will, reinforcing the bond between the creator and the creation.

The daily prayers, or Salat, are particularly significant in the life of a Muslim, serving as constant reminders of Allah's presence and sovereignty. Through prayer, Muslims renew their surrender to Allah's will, seeking guidance, strength, and forgiveness. The act of prostration during prayer symbolizes the ultimate submission, where the believer physically lowers themselves before God in humility and devotion.

Navigating Life's Trials with Faith

The Quran and the Hadith (sayings of Prophet Muhammad) address the human experience of suffering, hardship, and uncertainty, offering insights into how to navigate these challenges through surrender. Muslims are encouraged to see life's trials as tests of faith, opportunities for growth, and means to draw closer to Allah. Patience (Sabr) and gratitude (Shukr) are virtues highly esteemed in Islam, teaching believers to accept Allah's decree with a heart full of faith, whether in times of joy or adversity.

Islamic teachings on surrender extend beyond personal piety to encompass social justice, community service, and the stewardship of the earth. Muslims are called to implement Allah's guidance in every aspect of their lives, working towards the betterment of society and the environment. This holistic approach to surrender seeks not only personal salvation but also the welfare of the entire creation.

In the fast-paced, often fragmented modern world, the Islamic principle of living in surrender to Allah's will presents a profound and holistic approach to life that transcends the prevailing cultural narratives of autonomy and individualism. This principle infuses every aspect of a Muslim's life with meaning, from the mundane to the monumental, guiding not only personal and spiritual practices but also influencing societal values and ethical frameworks.

The essence of this surrender is not passive; rather, it is a dynamic and active engagement with the world through the lens of faith. Muslims are encouraged to navigate the complexities of contemporary life with a compass grounded in divine guidance, finding balance between the demands of the modern world and the timeless teachings of Islam. This balance is achieved by integrating Islamic principles into education, work, social justice, and community service, thereby manifesting one's faith in actions that contribute positively to society.

In environments where the pursuit of personal freedom and self-expression often leads to isolation and disconnection, Islam's emphasis on community and collective welfare offers a different paradigm. The concept of Ummah, or the global community of Muslims, exemplifies this, fostering a sense of unity and mutual support that transcends geographical, racial, and cultural divides. This communal aspect of surrender underscores the importance of caring for the needy, advocating for justice, and working towards the common good, reinforcing the idea that one's fulfilment is deeply connected to the well-being of others.

Moreover, Islamic teachings on surrender challenge the modern notion of freedom as the absence of constraints, proposing instead that true freedom lies in submission to Allah's will. This submission liberates individuals from the tyranny of their desires and the fleeting satisfactions of the material world, guiding them towards lasting peace and contentment. By surrendering their will to Allah, Muslims embrace a freedom that is spiritual in nature, marked by inner tranquillity and a deep connection to the divine.

Living surrender in the modern world also involves a continuous process of reflection, repentance, and renewal. Muslims are encouraged to regularly examine their actions and intentions, realigning themselves with God's will through prayer, fasting, and the study of the Quran. This spiritual discipline helps believers maintain their focus on the ultimate purpose of life, navigating the challenges and distractions of the contemporary age with grace and resilience.

Islam's teachings on surrender, deeply rooted in the Quran and the life of the Prophet Muhammad, thus offer a comprehensive framework for living a fulfilled and meaningful life in today's world. Through surrender to Allah's will, Muslims discover a source of strength, guidance, and comfort that empowers them to face the complexities of modern existence with confidence and hope. This path of surrender, characterized by deep faith, conscientious obedience, and heartfelt devotion, continues to inspire Muslims around the globe, offering profound insights into the pursuit of true freedom and the quest for spiritual fulfilment.

****

As we have now explored the profound themes of surrender within the major religious traditions, I want you to understand the universal essence that underpins these spiritual paths. It is not about the labels we assign to ourselves—be it Muslim, Christian, Sikh or any other—It is about recognising the core principles that resonate across these faiths. Surrender, in its many forms, is a fundamental human experience, a shared spiritual

55

heritage that transcends doctrinal differences. It is about yielding to something greater than ourselves, finding peace in the relinquishment of control, and discovering a deeper sense of purpose and connection through this act of faith. This exploration is not meant to delineate boundaries but to bridge them, highlighting the common ground upon which we all stand. It is a reminder that at the heart of many spiritual teachings lies a call to surrender—be it to God's will, to the divine plan, or to the unfolding flow of life itself. This surrender is not a sign of weakness but a source of strength, offering a path to understanding, peace, and ultimate fulfilment.

Now, let's explore beyond these global pillars of faith to delve into Indigenous and Shamanic Traditions. Here, we will discover concepts of surrender to nature and the interconnected web of life, as experienced by various indigenous cultures around the world. These traditions offer unique perspectives on surrender, emphasizing harmony with the natural world, the community, and the cosmos. Through this exploration, we hope to further expand our understanding of surrender, highlighting its universal relevance and the diverse ways it is manifested across human cultures. By weaving together these threads of wisdom, we aim to create a tapestry that reflects the richness and diversity of human spirituality. In doing so, we invite you to see surrender not just as a religious principle but as a universal spiritual practice, one that has the power to transform, heal, and connect us more deeply with the essence of who we truly are and with the world around us.

Indigenous Perspectives on Surrender

Indigenous cultures, with their profound connection to the land and the natural world, embody principles of surrender that teach us about balance, reciprocity, and respect for all living beings. For many Indigenous peoples, life is a sacred circle in which humans are but one part of a larger, interconnected community that includes animals, plants, the earth, and the spirit world. Living in surrender to this interconnectedness means recognising the mutual dependencies that sustain life and the responsibilities humans have to maintain these delicate balances.

In Indigenous worldviews, surrender is often manifested through practices and rituals that honour the earth, the seasons, and the cycles of life and death. These practices are not mere acts of worship but acts of deep listening and learning from the natural world, understanding its rhythms, and aligning human activities with them. This alignment requires a surrender of human ego and an acknowledgment that humans are not masters of the earth but participants in its harmony.

Shamanic Traditions and Surrender

Shamanic traditions, found in various forms across many Indigenous cultures, offer another lens through which to view surrender. Shamans act as mediators between the human world and the spirit world, navigating these realms to bring back wisdom, healing, and guidance for their communities. Their work involves a profound surrender to the spirits and forces they engage with, trusting in the guidance they receive and respecting the sovereignty of the non-human beings they interact with.

Surrender in shamanic practice is also about letting go of the ordinary constraints of ego and reality to enter altered states of consciousness, where deeper truths and connections can be revealed. This process is facilitated through rituals, plant medicines, drumming, chanting, and other practices that open the practitioner to experiences beyond the ordinary. The shaman's journey is a vivid example of surrender not as passivity but as an active, courageous engagement with the unseen and the unknown for the greater good of the community.

The Wisdom of Surrender in Nature

Both Indigenous and Shamanic traditions teach that surrender to the natural world and its laws is not a relinquishment of power but a way to access greater wisdom and strength. This wisdom teaches that humans are not separate from or superior to nature but are deeply embedded within it. Recognising and embracing this interconnectedness leads to a more sustainable, respectful, and fulfilling way of living on the earth.

Through the lens of these ancient traditions, surrender becomes a way to achieve a deeper harmony with the cosmos, a path to healing not only for individuals but for the planet itself. The concepts of surrender in Indigenous and Shamanic traditions—marked by reverence for nature, engagement with the spirit world, and a commitment to the communal web of life—offer valuable insights for our contemporary world. They remind us of the importance of listening to and learning from the natural world, urging us to rediscover our place within the great circle of life and to live in a way that honours all our relations.

In embracing these teachings, we find a universal call to surrender that transcends cultural and spiritual boundaries, inviting us to engage more deeply with the world around us and to find our own paths to balance, healing, and interconnectedness.

This deep immersion into Indigenous and Shamanic traditions enriches our understanding of surrender, presenting it as an essential principle that fosters harmony between humans and the natural world. By observing and embodying these ancient practices, we are reminded of the intrinsic value of living in accordance with the cycles and wisdom of nature. It encourages a shift from viewing the environment as a resource to be exploited, to seeing it as a sacred community to which we belong and for which we carry a responsibility.

The act of surrender, as illustrated through these traditions, is not merely about yielding to an external force; It is about recognising our innermost connections to that force and the reciprocal relationships that sustain life. This perspective challenges the contemporary narrative of dominance over nature, proposing instead a model of coexistence that honours the sanctity of all living beings.

In a world facing environmental crises, the insights offered by Indigenous and Shamanic traditions on surrender to nature's rhythms and laws are more relevant than ever. These teachings urge us to reconsider our lifestyles, values, and the impact of our actions on the planet. By adopting a stance of humility and respect towards the earth, we can begin to heal the wounds inflicted by centuries of disregard for our natural environment.

Moreover, the concept of surrender in these traditions offers a pathway to personal and collective transformation. It teaches that true strength lies in our ability to listen, learn, and adapt to the forces of life that move around and within us. In doing so, we open ourselves to a richer, more connected existence, grounded in the understanding that we are part of a much larger story that encompasses all of creation.

As we continue to explore the diverse expressions of surrender across cultures and spiritual paths, let us carry forward the wisdom of Indigenous and Shamanic traditions. Their reverence for the interconnected web of life offers a beacon of hope and a call to action, inviting us to live with greater awareness, compassion, and solidarity with the natural world. In embracing this call, we join an ancient and ongoing journey towards balance, harmony, and a deeper communion with the earth and each other.

Shamanic practices involving surrender to the spirit world for guidance and healing

Shamanic traditions, present in various cultures around the world, provide a fascinating insight into the practice of surrender, particularly in relation to the spirit world. These traditions hold that the visible world we inhabit is closely interwoven with a parallel realm inhabited by spirits—entities that can influence our lives in profound ways. Shamans, regarded as intermediaries between these two worlds, navigate the spirit realm to seek guidance, healing, and assistance for their communities. Their practices illustrate a profound form of surrender, one that requires trust, courage, and openness to the unknown.

Entering the Spirit World: The Shaman's Journey
The core of shamanic practice is the journey to the spirit world. This journey, often induced through drumming, dancing, fasting, or the use of entheogens, requires the shaman to surrender their ordinary perceptions of reality. In this altered state of consciousness, shamans are said to

communicate with spirit guides, ancestors, and other entities, seeking wisdom and knowledge that can benefit the physical world. This process is a vivid demonstration of surrender, as the shaman places complete trust in the spirits and the guidance they provide, relinquishing control and allowing the journey to unfold as it will.

Healing and the Power of Surrender

Shamanic healing practices are deeply rooted in the concept of surrender. Shamans believe that many illnesses have spiritual causes, such as soul loss or spiritual blockages. Healing involves surrendering to the spirits, allowing them to work through the shaman to restore balance and harmony to the afflicted individual. This may involve retrieving lost parts of the soul, removing harmful spiritual entities, or conveying messages from the spirit world. Both the shaman and the person receiving healing must surrender to the process, trusting in the power and wisdom of the spirits for restoration and wellbeing.

The Role of Rituals and Offerings

Rituals and offerings are another important aspect of shamanic practice, embodying the principle of surrender. These acts demonstrate respect and gratitude towards the spirits, acknowledging their power and seeking their favour. By making offerings of food, tobacco, or other substances, shamans surrender something of value to the spirit world, fostering a relationship of reciprocity and mutual respect. Rituals, whether they mark significant life transitions or seasonal changes, help to align the community with the rhythms of the natural and spiritual worlds, reinforcing the interconnectedness of all things.

Learning from the Spirits: Surrender as a Path to Knowledge
One of the most profound aspects of shamanic surrender is the openness to learning from the spirits. Shamans act as vessels for spiritual knowledge, surrendering their own ego and preconceptions to receive the teachings of the spirit world. This wisdom is then brought back to the community, offering insights into living in harmony with nature, resolving conflicts, and understanding the mysteries of existence. The shaman's role exemplifies how surrender can lead to enlightenment, healing, and the strengthening of communal bonds.

Contemporary Relevance of Shamanic Surrender
In today's world, where many feel disconnected from nature and the deeper aspects of existence, shamanic practices offer a reminder of the value of surrender to forces beyond our immediate understanding. They teach us that true healing, wisdom, and strength come from acknowledging our interconnectedness with the larger web of life and the spiritual dimensions that influence it. By embracing the principles of shamanic surrender, individuals can discover new paths to healing, personal growth, and a more profound engagement with the world around them.

Shamanic traditions, with their deep respect for the spirit world and the practice of surrender, provide a unique perspective on the journey towards wholeness and harmony. By learning to navigate the unseen realms with trust and humility, shamans remind us that there is much more to reality than meets the eye, and that by surrendering to the greater flows of existence, we can uncover deeper truths and find healing on multiple levels. Shamanic traditions across diverse cultures illuminate a path of profound surrender to the spirit world, offering guidance, healing, and a deeper connection to the fabric of the universe. In these practices, the act of surrender transcends mere acceptance, evolving into a dynamic engagement with forces and entities beyond our usual perception.

The journey into the spirit world, a cornerstone of shamanic practice, represents a profound form of surrender. This journey often requires the shaman to transcend ordinary states of consciousness, reaching into realms inhabited by spirits and ancestors who guide and protect their communities. Such journeys are facilitated through various means—ritualistic drumming, sacred plant medicines, fasting, and vigils—each method serving to alter the shaman's consciousness. Here, the shaman fully surrenders to the experience, allowing the spirit guides to lead the way. This trust is not given lightly; it is a testament to the shaman's faith in the spirit world's benevolence and wisdom.

In the realm of healing, shamans engage deeply with the concept of surrender. They understand that many illnesses stem from spiritual imbalances or disharmonies, which might manifest as physical or emotional symptoms. Healing rituals often involve the shaman surrendering to the spirits, allowing them to work through the shaman to effect change in the physical world. This could involve soul retrieval, where parts of the individual's essence are brought back from the spirit world, or cleansing rituals to remove negative energies. Both healer and healed enter these practices with a spirit of surrender, trusting in the healing knowledge and power of the spirits.

Shamanic rituals and the act of making offerings represent another layer of surrender. These acts are expressions of respect and gratitude towards the spirits, acknowledging their power and influence. Offerings—whether they are objects, songs, dances, or prayers—are given to honour the spirits and ask for their continued guidance and protection. Such rituals reinforce the bonds between the physical and spirit worlds, embodying a mutual exchange that maintains balance and harmony.

Learning from the spirits embodies the ultimate surrender to the unseen forces of the world. Shamans, as intermediaries, relinquish their own ego and personal desires to become conduits for spiritual wisdom. This wisdom, once brought back from the spirit journeys, is shared with the community, offering insights into living in balance with nature, resolving personal and collective issues, and understanding life's deeper meanings. The shaman's role highlights how surrender to the spirit world opens pathways to profound knowledge and communal well-being.

In contemporary times, where disconnection from nature and spiritual realms can feel pervasive, the principles of shamanic surrender offer vital lessons. They remind us of the importance of acknowledging and engaging with the unseen aspects of our world, suggesting that true wisdom, healing, and strength lie in our ability to trust in and align with forces greater than ourselves. By embracing these ancient practices of surrender, we can rediscover our interconnectedness with all of life, finding paths to personal healing and a deeper engagement with the world.

Shamanic traditions, with their reverence for the intricate dance between the seen and unseen, teach us that surrender is not a passive act but a courageous step into a broader understanding of existence. Through this surrender, we open ourselves to the wisdom of the spirit world, finding guidance and healing that transcend our physical realities and connect us more deeply with the universal web of life.

As we journey further into the exploration of surrender across different cultures and spiritual landscapes, we now turn our attention towards the profound teachings of Eastern philosophies and religions. Here, in the contemplative depths of Taoism and Zen Buddhism, surrender unfolds in unique and enlightening ways. These traditions offer insightful perspectives on how surrendering to the natural flow of life and detaching from personal desires can lead to profound peace and understanding.

Taoism, with its principle of Wu Wei, and Zen Buddhism, with its emphasis on mindfulness and the release of attachments, both advocate for a way of life that is in harmony with the essence of existence. These paths teach us the value of letting go, of embracing the moment as it is, and of finding the extraordinary within the ordinary. Through their practices and teachings, we are invited to explore surrender not just as a concept, but as a lived experience that can offer freedom, clarity, and a deeper connection with the world around us.

In this exploration, we will delve into the heart of these Eastern traditions, uncovering the wisdom they hold about the nature of surrender and the paths they offer towards a life of harmony and enlightenment.

Eastern Philosophies and Religions: The Harmony of Surrender

As we journey further into our exploration of surrender across spiritual traditions, we pivot towards the rich landscapes of Eastern philosophies and religions. Here, the concepts of surrender are articulated with nuanced understanding and profound depth, particularly within Taoism and Zen Buddhism. These traditions offer unique perspectives on how surrendering to the natural flow of life and the relinquishing of personal desires lead to harmony and enlightenment.

Taoism, an ancient Chinese philosophy and spiritual path, introduces the principle of Wu Wei, often translated as 'non-action' or 'effortless action.' This concept is not about inaction but about aligning one's will with the Tao, or the fundamental nature of the universe, to act in harmony with everything that exists. Wu Wei embodies a form of surrender to the Tao, advocating for a life lived in accordance with the natural order and rhythms, free from forced effort and unnecessary strife.

In Zen Buddhism, another profound Eastern tradition, the emphasis is placed on mindfulness, meditation, and the practice of letting go of attachments. This form of surrender involves releasing the grip on our thoughts, emotions, and the insistent ego, to embrace the present moment fully. Through the cultivation of awareness and the discipline of detachment, practitioners learn to navigate the vicissitudes of life with grace and equanimity, reflecting a deep surrender to the unfolding experience of being.

Both Taoism and Zen Buddhism, through their respective teachings on Wu Wei and mindfulness, guide individuals toward a deeper understanding of surrender. This surrender is not a resignation but an active engagement with life's inherent wisdom and the acceptance of its impermanent nature. It is a journey toward inner peace and realisation, facilitated by the gentle relinquishing of control and the harmonious alignment with the way things are.

These Eastern philosophies and religions, with their emphasis on harmony, naturalness, and the middle way, contribute significantly to the global tapestry of spiritual insight on surrender. They offer pathways to liberation that are both accessible and profound, inviting us to explore the depths of our being and our relationship with the universe. Through the principles of Wu Wei and mindfulness, we are reminded that true strength and freedom lie in our ability to let go and trust in the natural course of existence.

The teachings of Taoism and Zen Buddhism, focusing on Wu Wei and mindfulness, respectively, present a form of surrender that is both liberating and enlightening. This surrender involves a deep trust in the natural process of life, encouraging a flow with existence rather than against it. It is through this harmonious alignment that one finds true peace and fulfilment.

Taoism and the Art of Wu Wei

Wu Wei, a central tenet of Taoism, encourages acting in accord with the Tao, the underlying principle that governs all life. This doesn't imply passivity but rather an informed non-action, a choice to not act against the natural grain of events. Practitioners of Wu Wei understand that often the most effective action is to stay still, to observe, and to allow things to unfold in their own time. This concept teaches that force and effort can disrupt the natural harmony of the world, leading to resistance and conflict. Instead, by embracing Wu Wei, one surrenders personal agendas, adopting a stance of openness and flexibility that allows for the Tao to manifest the best outcomes.

Zen Buddhism: Mindfulness and Letting Go

In Zen Buddhism, surrender is intricately linked with mindfulness and the practice of letting go of attachments. This path encourages a keen awareness of the present moment, free from the distractions of past regrets or future anxieties. Such surrender involves a radical acceptance of the present as it is, without superimposition of personal desires or fears. Practitioners learn to observe their thoughts and emotions without judgment or attachment, understanding that these are transient and not the essence of their true nature. Through meditation and mindful living, Zen Buddhism teaches how to surrender the ego, allowing individuals to experience life more fully and to respond to the world around them with compassion and wisdom.

Harmonious Living through Surrender

Both Taoism and Zen Buddhism offer profound insights into the nature of existence and the role of the individual within it. They teach that resistance to life's flow and clinging to personal desires lead to disharmony and suffering. Conversely, surrendering to the natural order, whether it is the Tao or the present moment, brings about a state of harmony and ease. This ease is not born out of ignorance or avoidance of life's challenges but from a deep understanding and acceptance of life as it unfolds.

These Eastern traditions remind us that the art of surrender is not about giving up our power but about realising where true power lies—in harmony with the forces larger than ourselves. It is a journey of discovering the strength in vulnerability, the wisdom in simplicity, and the freedom in letting go. As we integrate these teachings into our lives, we learn to navigate our existence with a greater sense of peace, balance, and alignment with the universal truths that govern all life.

The paths offered by Taoism and Zen Buddhism enrich our understanding of surrender, showing it to be a vital practice for achieving a profound sense of connection with the world and our place within it. By adopting the principles of Wu Wei and mindfulness, we open ourselves to a more fluid and responsive way of being, one that embraces the full spectrum of human experience with grace and equanimity.

This deep appreciation of surrender within Eastern philosophies illuminates a transformative approach to life, one that emphasizes harmony, balance, and the natural flow of existence. As we absorb the lessons from Taoism and Zen Buddhism, we uncover a universal wisdom that speaks to the heart of what it means to live fully and authentically.

Integrating Eastern Wisdom into Daily Life

The principles of Wu Wei and mindfulness offer more than just philosophical insight; they provide practical guidance for living in harmony with ourselves and the world around us. By practicing Wu Wei, we learn the value of patience, timing, and the power of subtle influence rather than forceful action. This approach encourages us to be more attuned to the rhythms of nature and the dynamics of our relationships, fostering an environment where growth and success occur naturally.

Similarly, the practice of mindfulness cultivated in Zen Buddhism teaches us to live with full awareness and presence. This heightened state of consciousness brings clarity and insight, helping us to make wiser decisions and to respond to life's challenges with compassion and equanimity.

Mindfulness becomes a tool for navigating the complexities of modern existence, enabling us to find peace amidst chaos and connection in moments of isolation.

The Global Relevance of Surrender

The teachings of Taoism and Zen Buddhism on surrender hold profound relevance in our contemporary world. In an age marked by rapid change, environmental crises, and social upheaval, these ancient wisdoms offer a beacon of hope and a path toward sustainable living. They remind us that true progress and well-being are achieved not through domination and control but through harmony and cooperation with the natural world.

Moreover, the emphasis on inner peace and personal growth found in these traditions provides a counterpoint to the materialism and consumerism that often characterize modern life. By valuing simplicity, contentment, and mindfulness, we can cultivate a more fulfilling and meaningful existence, one that prioritizes the well-being of the whole over the desires of the individual.

The Universal Call to Surrender

As we conclude our exploration of surrender within Eastern philosophies and religions, we are reminded of the profound interconnectedness of all spiritual traditions. Whether through the Taoist practice of Wu Wei or the Zen Buddhist approach to mindfulness, the call to surrender emerges as a universal theme, uniting us in our search for harmony, understanding, and peace.

These teachings encourage us to embrace life's uncertainties with an open heart, to find strength in vulnerability, and to seek wisdom in the simplicity of being. They invite us to participate in the ongoing dance of existence with grace and joy, trusting in the journey and the myriad ways it unfolds.

By incorporating the essence of surrender into our lives, we align ourselves with a timeless wisdom that transcends cultural and religious boundaries. It is a wisdom that offers guidance, healing, and a deeper connection to the world, calling us to live in harmony with the profound truths that underlie our shared human experience.

Modern Interpretations and Movements

As we transition from the ancient and traditional to the contemporary, we enter a realm where spiritual concepts evolve and adapt to the rhythms of modern life. This next stage of our exploration takes us into the diverse and dynamic world of modern interpretations and movements, where the age-old theme of surrender finds new expressions and meanings. In this era of rapid technological advancement and global connectivity, the ways in which individuals understand and practice surrender have expanded, blending traditional wisdom with new insights and approaches.

This phase of our journey illuminates how contemporary society grapples with the notion of surrender, not just as a spiritual or religious act, but as a transformative principle that permeates various aspects of human existence. The rise of New Age spirituality and the integration of psychological perspectives into the discourse on surrender reflect a growing collective desire to reconcile the spiritual with the practical, the ancient with the modern.

In this context, surrender is reimagined and reinterpreted, offering pathways to personal growth, healing, and a deeper connection with the cosmos. These modern movements and interpretations invite us to consider surrender not only in relation to a divine will or cosmic order but also as an essential practice for self-realisation and psychological wellbeing. They propose that surrender, whether it is to the Universe, a higher self, or the processes of our own psyche, can lead to profound insights, liberation from self-imposed limitations, and a more authentic and fulfilling life.

As we delve into these modern interpretations and movements, we'll explore how contemporary thinkers, spiritual leaders, and seekers navigate the concept of surrender, adapting ancient wisdom to address the challenges and opportunities of the 21st century. This exploration offers a unique lens through which to view the enduring relevance of surrender, revealing its capacity to inspire change, foster resilience, and cultivate a sense of harmony and peace in an ever-changing world.

In the landscape of contemporary spirituality, the rise of New Age movements marks a significant shift in how surrender is conceptualized and practiced. This broad and eclectic domain draws from a myriad of spiritual traditions, blending Eastern philosophies, mysticism, and Western esoteric thought to forge a holistic view of the human experience. Within this framework, surrender becomes an act of alignment with the Universe or a higher self, transcending traditional religious confines to embrace a more personal and experiential approach to spirituality.

New Age spirituality posits that the Universe operates on principles of harmony and abundance, and that individuals, by aligning their intentions and actions with these principles, can tap into a flow of cosmic energy. Surrender, in this context, is about letting go of resistance—be it fear, doubt, or attachment—and trusting in the benevolent guidance of a higher intelligence. It is a conscious choice to open oneself to the flow of life, embracing both its light and shadow aspects with equanimity and openness. This form of surrender is seen as a pathway to awakening, a means to transcend the ego and connect with a more authentic and empowered self.

Parallel to the spiritual narratives within New Age thought, contemporary psychological perspectives offer a nuanced understanding of surrender as a means to personal growth and overcoming ego. Psychology, with its deep dive into the human psyche, recognise s the transformative potential of surrendering control and embracing vulnerability. From this vantage point, surrender is not about defeat but about acknowledging the limitations of the ego and the futility of clinging to rigid self-conceptions and outcomes.

Therapeutic practices and mindfulness techniques emphasize the importance of surrender in healing and self-discovery. By learning to let go of the need for control, individuals can navigate life's uncertainties with greater flexibility and resilience, opening themselves to new experiences and perspectives. This psychological approach to surrender involves a delicate balance between acceptance and agency, inviting individuals to engage with their lives actively while being open to change and growth.

Both New Age spirituality and contemporary psychology enrich the discourse on surrender, offering insights that resonate with the challenges and aspirations of modern individuals. They provide tools and practices for navigating the complexities of life in a way that is both grounded and transcendent, practical and spiritual. This convergence of ancient wisdom and modern understanding underscores the timeless relevance of surrender as a fundamental aspect of the human condition, inviting us to explore its depths and discover its transformative power.

As we reflect on these modern interpretations and movements, it becomes clear that the art of surrender is as varied and complex as the tapestry of human experience itself. Whether through spiritual exploration or psychological inquiry, surrender emerges as a key to unlocking a richer, more meaningful existence. It challenges us to question, to explore, and ultimately, to open ourselves to the myriad possibilities that life offers. In doing so, we find that surrender, in all its forms, is not a relinquishing of power but a profound embrace of life's true potential.

This exploration into the modern realms of spirituality and psychology reveals that surrender, a concept as old as humanity itself, retains its potency and relevance in the contemporary world, adapting to new understandings and contexts. The dialogue between ancient spiritual wisdom and modern psychological insights has birthed a nuanced perspective on surrender, one that embraces both its mystical and practical dimensions.

The Journey Within: Surrender and Self-Discovery

At the heart of both New Age spirituality and psychological approaches is the journey towards self-discovery and self-realisation. Surrender is identified as a crucial step in this journey, a doorway to deeper self-awareness and transformation. In the New Age context, this often involves tuning into the intuition and inner wisdom that guide individuals towards their true purpose and potential. Surrender becomes an act of faith in the self's capacity to connect with the universal energies and wisdom that support growth and fulfilment.

Psychology, with its emphasis on introspection and therapeutic healing, views surrender as a necessary process for overcoming the barriers erected by the ego. Through surrender, individuals can confront and release deep-seated fears, traumas, and limiting beliefs, paving the way for healing and personal evolution. This process is facilitated by mindfulness practices, therapy, and other reflective activities that encourage individuals to embrace their vulnerabilities and accept their authentic selves.

The Role of Community and Connection

Another dimension of surrender in the modern context is the recognition of the importance of community and collective experience. New Age spirituality often highlights the interconnectedness of all life, urging individuals to see themselves as part of a larger whole. Surrender, in this sense, involves releasing the illusion of separateness and embracing a sense of unity with others and the natural world. This perspective fosters a sense of belonging and connection, which is crucial for personal and collective wellbeing.

Similarly, contemporary psychological practices acknowledge the therapeutic value of community and social support. Group therapy, community mindfulness practices, and support groups are spaces where individuals can experience the power of collective surrender—sharing vulnerabilities, learning from others' experiences, and supporting each other's growth. This communal aspect of surrender underscores the human need for connection and the healing that comes from being seen and supported by others.

Navigating Challenges with Grace

In facing the complexities and uncertainties of modern life, the concept of surrender offers a strategy for navigating challenges with grace and resilience. Rather than resisting change or adversity, surrender invites individuals to flow with life's changes, finding strength in adaptability and openness. This approach does not negate the reality of suffering or hardship but offers a way to move through these experiences with a sense of peace and purpose.

The Evolving Landscape of Surrender

The modern interpretations and movements surrounding surrender illustrate its evolving landscape, reflecting humanity's continuous search for meaning, connection, and peace. By weaving together, the threads of spiritual wisdom and psychological insight, we gain a richer, more complex understanding of surrender—one that honours its roots while embracing the challenges and opportunities of the present.

As we move forward, the teachings of New Age spirituality and contemporary psychology serve as beacons, guiding us towards a deeper engagement with the world and ourselves. In this light, surrender emerges not just as a spiritual or psychological concept but as a lived practice, a way of being that embraces the fullness of the human experience with courage, openness, and love. Through this embrace, we find that surrender, in all its forms, offers a path to liberation and fulfilment, illuminating the way to a more harmonious and awakened life.

In exploring the depths of human wisdom and the quest for inner peace, we encounter timeless truths that transcend cultural and historical boundaries. One such truth is encapsulated in the phrase 'everything is as it should be.' This simple yet profound statement, echoing the teachings of Sikhism, Buddhism, Hinduism, and countless other spiritual and philosophical traditions, reminds us of the power of acceptance, trust, and surrender to the unfolding of life. It is a reminder borne of collective human insight, a distillation of the understanding that, despite the complexities and challenges of our existence, there is an inherent order and purpose to the universe. As we reflect on this wisdom, let us consider it not the legacy of a single individual but a gift from the collective human spirit, offering guidance, comfort, and the courage to embrace life's journey with an open heart.

Chapter 2: Signs and Synchronicities

I have always been a firm believer in signs. Even as a child, I found myself whispering into the universe, "If I see a shooting star, then it means my wish will come true," or "I will ace my exam." This habit of seeking and interpreting signs from the world around me has been a constant companion throughout my life. It was a way of making sense of the universe, a method to gauge the unseen forces at play, guiding me through the maze of everyday existence.

My journey with signs has been a faithful companion, evolving from childhood whimsies into a profound spiritual practice. As a child, the universe seemed like a grand magician, ready to reveal its secrets through the simplest of signs—a falling leaf, a randomly found feather, or the unexpected appearance of a rainbow. These were my early conversations with the cosmos, innocent yet deeply felt attempts to understand the world beyond my immediate senses. The journey into spiritual literature, encountering transformative works like "The Power" by Rhonda Byrne and the insightful teachings of Gabby Bernstein, was like finding a map to a territory I had always known it existed but hadn't fully explored. These writings validated my intuitions and experiences, affirming that the universe does indeed communicate in subtle but significant ways. The idea that we can co-create our reality with the universe by understanding and responding to these signs was both empowering and awe-inspiring.

However, the path of belief in signs is not devoid of its shadows. Consider the reader who, much like myself, has looked to the skies for confirmation of a new job, only to face rejection, or the one who finds feathers on their path, interpreting them as signs of a looming spiritual awakening, only to encounter mundane challenges that seem to contradict every sign received. These moments of apparent dissonance between our interpretations of signs and the unfolding of events can sow seeds of doubt, testing the strength of our faith.

Yet, it is precisely within these moments of doubt and seeming contradiction that the deepest lessons of surrender and trust are learned. The journey taught me, and perhaps you, the reader, that the power of signs lies not in their ability to predict outcomes or provide clear-cut answers. Instead, their true power is in guiding us towards a deeper engagement with the flow of life, encouraging us to trust in the journey even when the destination remains unclear.

Embracing the belief in signs and synchronicities invites us into a dance with the cosmos, where each step, each sign, is part of a broader dialogue between our souls and the universe. It is a dialogue that requires listening with the heart, interpreting with the soul, and, most importantly, surrendering to the wisdom that the universe imparts through its myriad languages.

The transition from seeking signs as validations of our desires to recognising them as sacred communications marks a profound evolution in our spiritual path. This shift challenges us to expand our perception, to see beyond the surface of our immediate wants, and to attune ourselves to a more profound dialogue with the universe. It invites us to consider the possibility that every sign, every synchronicity, is a thread in a larger weave of divine conversation, one that speaks to the growth of our souls, the challenges we need to overcome, and the direction we are meant to follow.

In this deeper engagement with the language of the cosmos, we begin to understand that signs are not random or merely coincidental. They are the universe's way of guiding us, of showing us that we are not alone in our journey. Each sign, whether it appears as a recurring number, a song that plays at just the right moment, or an animal that crosses our path, carries a message tailored to our journey, a nudge towards reflection and, ultimately, growth. These signs ask us to look inward, to question our current paths, and to consider new directions that might lead us closer to our true selves and our purpose in this world.

Belief in signs and synchronicities thus becomes a practice of faith and attentiveness. It requires us to cultivate a listening heart, one that is open to receiving and interpreting the universe's messages. This practice does not demand blind faith but rather an active engagement with our intuition and a willingness to see the interconnectedness of all things. It is about learning to trust the process, to understand that the universe has its timing, and that what we need will come to us when we are ready to receive it.

Navigating this journey with belief in signs and synchronicities enriches our lives with a deeper sense of meaning and connection. It transforms our relationship with the universe from one of separation and isolation to one of partnership and dialogue. This partnership doesn't remove the challenges of life but equips us with a broader perspective to approach them, fostering resilience, patience, and a deeper trust in the flow of life.

As we delve deeper into this exploration of signs and synchronicities, we are not merely seeking answers or looking for guidance in isolation. We are learning to participate in a cosmic dance that has been unfolding since the beginning of time, awakening to the subtle whispers of the universe that surround us. This shared journey of awakening promises a transformation that transcends the personal, tapping into the collective heartbeat of existence itself. It invites us to a renewed sense of wonder and alignment with the greater forces that animate our world, opening our eyes to the magic and mystery that life offers to those willing to see with the heart and listen with the soul.

In the tapestry of our lives, the universe whispers to us through signs and synchronicities, a subtle language that, when listened to, guides, warns, and enlightens us on our journey. Recognising these signs, understanding their meanings, and integrating their messages into our lives can transform our relationship with the cosmos, deepening our connection to the unseen forces that guide our path.

One afternoon, while wrestling with a crucial life decision, I found myself walking through a park, lost in thought. My gaze fell upon a solitary dandelion, standing resilient amidst the grass. As a child, I believed dandelions held magic—blow on them, make a wish, and watch your dreams carry into the wind. In that moment, the dandelion was a sign from the universe: to let go, to trust in the winds of change. This personal anecdote echoes the wisdom found in Paulo Coelho's The Alchemist, where the protagonist learns to read the omens scattered along his path, each one a guidepost steering him towards his destiny.

The universe communicates in myriad ways—through numbers, patterns, animals, and even the random conversations we overhear. Recognising these signs begins with cultivating an openness and receptivity to the world around us. It is about tuning into the frequency of the universe, where every coincidence is a potential message, every anomaly a lesson waiting to be understood. As Carl

Jung, the Swiss psychiatrist who coined the term 'synchronicity,' observed, "Synchronicity is an ever-present reality for those who have eyes to see."

But how do we differentiate between a genuine sign and the mere noise of life? The key lies in intuition—the silent voice within that knows without knowing why. When we encounter a sign, it often comes with a sense of inner knowing, a resonance that feels undeniably significant. It is a moment of recognition, where something within us clicks, and we understand, even if we can't quite explain it.

Interpreting signs is as much an art as it is a science. It requires a balance between openness to the mysteries of the universe and discernment in deciphering their relevance to our lives. A helpful practice is to keep a journal of these occurrences, noting when they happen, how they made you feel, and any subsequent outcomes. Over time, patterns emerge, and the language of the universe becomes clearer, more familiar.

Gabby Bernstein, in her book The Universe Has Your Back, emphasizes the importance of asking for clear signs and being specific about what you seek guidance on. This act of asking not only sets our intention out into the universe but also primes us to receive and recognise the answers when they come.

In embracing the journey of recognising and interpreting signs, we embark on a dialogue with the universe, a conversation that spans the breadth of existence. It is a process that invites us to trust more deeply in the flow of life, to surrender to the unknown with faith that we are supported and guided every step of the way. Through this practice, we uncover not just guidance for our paths but a deeper understanding of the interconnectedness of all things.

As we open ourselves to the language of the universe, let us remember the words of Rumi: "The universe is not outside of you. Look inside yourself; everything that you want, you already are." In recognising signs and synchronicities, we are reminded of our own inner wisdom and the profound truth that we are intimately connected to the vast, unfolding mystery of existence.

Understanding and interpreting signs from the universe involves delving into the subtle, often nuanced language that transcends words, manifesting instead through symbols, synchronicities, and events that seem too pointed to be mere coincidences. To truly grasp the essence of these signs, especially in the throes of life's most challenging periods, requires a blend of openness, intuition, and a willingness to see beyond the superficial layers of our experiences.

In the complexity of our lives, signs serve as guideposts, whispering directions, affirmations, or warnings in ways that resonate with our deepest selves. These signs, whether encountered during moments of uncertainty, decision-making, or personal turmoil, are the universe's way of communicating with us, offering insights and guidance tailored to our individual journeys. The art of recognising these signs lies in attuning ourselves to the subtleties of our environment and the inner workings of our intuition—a sense that something has been placed in our path for a reason.

Consider the moments when you are faced with a decision that feels insurmountable, where each option seems fraught with its own set of challenges. In such times, a sign might appear as an unexpected encounter with an old friend who brings a new perspective, a book that falls open to a page bearing poignant advice, or even a dream vivid enough to sway your feelings on the matter. These are not random occurrences but meaningful responses to the silent queries we cast into the universe.

The key to deciphering these messages lies in cultivating a state of openness. This doesn't mean looking for signs in every corner but rather maintaining an alertness to the unusual, the timely, and the resonant. It is about recognising when a pattern emerges from the randomness, signalling a message tailored for you. For instance, consistently seeing the same sequence of numbers, encountering specific animals, or stumbling upon recurring themes in conversations could be the universe's way of highlighting something that requires your attention.

Engaging with these signs demands a balance between scepticism and faith. It involves analysing the context of these occurrences with a critical mind while also trusting in the non-linear, symbolic language of the universe. This dual approach allows for a deeper engagement with the signs, where their meanings unfold not just through intellectual interpretation but through a felt sense of their significance.

Moreover, interpreting signs, particularly in life's darker moments, requires an understanding that the universe's guidance is not always direct or immediate. The clarity we seek might unfold gradually, with signs nudging us towards introspection, patience, or action, depending on what our growth necessitates at the time. For example, in the midst of grief or loss, a sign might not direct us towards quick resolution but rather encourage us to embrace our emotions, to find strength in vulnerability, indicating that healing is a journey rather than a destination.

The practice of recognising and interpreting signs is, at its core, a dialogue with the universe. It is a process that deepens our connection to the world around us and to the unseen forces that guide and shape our existence. By learning to listen to and trust in these signs, we open ourselves to a richer, more interconnected experience of life, one that acknowledges the mysterious and sacred dimensions that dance just beyond the edge of our everyday awareness. This dialogue with the universe becomes a source of guidance, comfort, and inspiration, especially when traversed with an open heart and a willing spirit.

In the realm of interpreting signs from the universe, the practice becomes particularly profound when we apply it to our personal narratives, especially during times of crisis or uncertainty. Let me share a story that illustrates the power of seeking and finding guidance through signs, a story that underscores the practical application of this spiritual practice in navigating life's challenges.

During a period of intense difficulty, where financial turmoil loomed large and the future seemed fraught with uncertainty, I found myself at a crossroads. An opportunity had presented itself, yet it was far from what I had envisioned for my path. Torn between holding out for something better and the pressing need to alleviate our financial strain, I sought clarity in the only way I knew—by turning to the universe for a sign. With a specific request, I asked the universe to present me with a red object, one that I could physically hold in my hand and find outside my home, as a signal to stay the course, to believe that the tides would turn in my favour if I just held on.

That evening, as I walked, entrenched in my thoughts and the weight of the decision ahead, my eyes were inexplicably drawn to the ground. There, amidst the ordinariness of the pavement, lay a red paper clip. The specificity of the object, its colour, and the fulfilment of my earlier stipulation struck me profoundly. What were the chances? In that moment, the paper clip was more than just a piece of metal; it was a beacon of hope, a direct communication from the universe assuring me that patience and faith were what was needed.

This experience, as simple as it may seem, encapsulates the essence of practical spirituality. It wasn't merely about finding a red object; it was about how that sign, in its timing and specificity, resonated with the deepest parts of my soul, offering guidance when it was most needed. The red paper clip became a symbol of trust, a reminder that the universe listens and responds in the most unexpected ways.

Interpreting this sign—and indeed, any sign—requires an openness to the symbolic language of the universe. It involves setting clear intentions, as I did with my request, but also being open to the outcome, understanding that signs are not a guarantee of results but a nudge in the right direction. They require us to trust not only in the universe but in our capacity to navigate the challenges before us, armed with the knowledge that we are supported in our journey.

In practical terms, working with signs means being both specific in our requests and flexible in our interpretations. It means recognising that while we might seek a particular outcome, the universe might guide us towards what we truly need, which may not always align with our initial desires. The red paper clip was a sign to persevere, but it was also a call to trust—to believe in the unseen forces at play and to find peace in the knowledge that everything unfolds in its perfect timing.

For those seeking to incorporate the practice of recognising and interpreting signs into their lives, especially during tough times, the key lies in balance. It is about finding the middle ground between seeking guidance and making autonomous decisions, between trusting in the universe and taking actionable steps towards our goals. It is a dance between destiny and free will, where signs serve as guideposts, illuminating the path but requiring us to walk it.

This story, and the countless others like it, serves as a testament to the power of surrender, of opening ourselves to the universe's wisdom, and of finding guidance in the most unassuming of signs. It reminds us that no matter the darkness we face, there is always a beacon of hope, a red paper clip on our path, waiting to be discovered, offering the assurance that we are never truly alone in our journey.

When navigating the mysterious terrain of signs and synchronicities, It is not uncommon to encounter scenarios where, despite receiving what appears to be a clear sign, the anticipated outcomes don't materialize as expected. Such moments can be perplexing, even disheartening, challenging our faith in the universe's guidance and in our ability to interpret the messages we receive. However, these situations also offer profound opportunities for growth and deeper understanding. Let's explore how one might navigate such a scenario, transforming confusion into clarity and trust.

Scenario: The Unfulfilled Sign

Imagine you are at a significant juncture in your life, perhaps contemplating a major career change. After asking the universe for a sign to confirm you are making the right decision, you encounter an unmistakable symbol—a billboard with a message so specific to your situation, it sends shivers down your spine. Taking this as a green light, you proceed with the change, only to find the path ahead fraught with challenges, the promised success nowhere in sight. The sign, so clear and promising, seems to have led you astray.

Step 1: Reflection and Reassessment

The first step in navigating this dissonance is to engage in deep reflection. Ask yourself:

What expectations did I attach to the sign? How might my interpretation have been influenced by my desires or fears? Is there a possibility that the sign was guiding me towards a lesson or growth opportunity, rather than a specific outcome?

This process of introspection can reveal underlying motivations and expectations that may have coloured your interpretation of the sign. It is an invitation to reassess not just the sign itself but your relationship with the guidance you seek from the universe.

Step 2: Embrace the Lesson

Every sign, fulfilled or not, carries a lesson. Perhaps the challenge you are facing is meant to foster resilience, develop new skills, or push you to explore avenues you wouldn't have considered otherwise. The key is to remain open to the possibility that the universe's plan for you might be broader and more intricate than you initially perceived.

Reflect on what this experience is teaching you about patience, trust, or letting go. Consider journaling about your journey, noting any insights or shifts in perspective that arise. This practice can transform seemingly unfulfilled signs into valuable stepping stones on your spiritual path.

Step 3: Cultivate Detachment

Detachment doesn't mean giving up on your goals or ignoring the signs you receive. Instead, It is about loosening your grip on the outcome, understanding that the true power of signs lies in their ability to guide us towards our highest good, which may not always align with our immediate wants.

Practice letting go of specific expectations and trust that, regardless of the immediate outcome, you are being led to where you need to be. Meditation and mindfulness exercises can aid in cultivating this sense of detachment, helping you stay cantered and open to the flow of life.

Step 4: Deepen Your Dialogue with the Universe

View the experience as an opportunity to deepen your dialogue with the universe. Continue to ask for guidance, but also express gratitude for the lessons learned, even when they come in unexpected packages. Strengthening this communication enhances your receptivity and sharpens your interpretive skills, making you more attuned to the signs and what they signify in your life.

Step 5: Take Inspired Action

Finally, remember that signs are not just about receiving but also about acting. Take inspired action based on the insights and lessons you have gleaned from the experience. This might mean adjusting your course, trying a new approach, or simply persevering with renewed faith.

Navigating the aftermath of an unfulfilled sign is a journey back to trust—not just in the universe but in your resilience and capacity to grow from every circumstance. It is a reminder that the journey is as significant as the destination, and that every step, every sign, is a part of the intricate dance of co-creation with the universe. Through this process, we learn not only to seek signs but to live them, embodying the wisdom they offer as we walk our path with courage, openness, and a heart ready to receive.

Also, I would like you to remember that you can always create your own signs and your own meanings. Rather than waiting for signs to appear, you can incorporate certain things into your day-to-day life to gain insights. This personal empowerment is at the heart of bridging the gap between the universe's guidance and the tools we might use to connect with it. Tarot cards became such a tool for me, a means of tapping into an intuitive understanding that I had once viewed with scepticism. The esoteric nature of tarot, initially at odds with my preference for tangible, clear-cut signs, began to fascinate me when I discovered Jayne Wallace's Oceanic Tarot deck. As a Pisces, I felt an intrinsic pull towards the water-themed imagery, which promised a unique way of connecting with the broader currents of the universe and the deep reservoir of my own intuition.

My approach to using tarot was unconventional at first. I viewed it more as a game, a way to test the waters of this new form of guidance. I would shuffle the deck and pay special attention to any cards that fell out during the process. For instance, if the Magician card slipped from my hands, I would place it back in the deck and shuffle again. If it reappeared, I took it as a sign that its message was meant for me. This playful method helped me build trust in the tarot as a tool for insight, allowing me to engage with it on my terms.

This personal journey with tarot taught me a valuable lesson about the nature of signs and guidance: It is deeply personal and infinitely customisable. Inspired by Rhonda Byrne's "The Power," I began to explore the idea of assigning my own meanings to colours, objects, and symbols, creating a personalized language of signs that resonated with my frequency and understanding. For example, green became my colour for success, reflecting growth and prosperity. Pink symbolized a high, positive frequency, while red warned me of lower, more challenging energies.

Through this practice, I became more attuned to the frequencies at which I was operating. If my surroundings seemed to flood with red, it was a clear indication that I needed to shift my mindset and elevate my frequency. Remarkably, as my awareness and intentions changed, so too did the colours that dominated my perception. Suddenly, pink hues began to surface more frequently, signalling an alignment with higher, more positive vibrations. This approach, whether through tarot cards or the personalized meanings of colours and symbols, underscores the profound flexibility and creativity in our communication with the universe. It reaffirms that the language of signs is not a one-size-fits-all but a deeply personal script that we can write and interpret in ways that speak directly to our hearts and circumstances. By engaging with these tools, we actively participate in the co-creation of our reality, attuning ourselves to the subtle energies and messages that guide us. This participation is not passive; It is a conscious act of openness, creativity, and trust. Whether It is the tarot card that falls out of the deck or the recurring appearance of specific colours and symbols, these signs invite us into a deeper exploration of our inner worlds and the universal forces that weave through our lives.

In sharing this personal narrative, I hope to explain the different ways we can connect with and interpret the guidance the universe offers us. Whether through tarot, the symbolism of colours, or any other method that resonates, the key lies in finding what speaks to you, trusting in the process, and remaining open to the transformations that this practice can bring. It is a journey of discovery, where the signs and symbols we encounter are not just guides but mirrors, reflecting our deepest selves and the infinite possibilities that await us when we choose to engage with the universe's vast and mysterious language.

Chapter 3: Angels and Their Role in Our Lives

In the unfolding story of our lives, there are forces, presences, some might call angels, that accompany us with a silent beat of wings or a whisper of spirit that we feel more than hear. Chapter 3 opens the door to a realm that might seem as intangible as a dream yet as real as the air we breathe—where beings of light and energy, known to many as angels, exist to guide, protect, and illuminate our paths.

Angels, in the tapestry of human belief, stretch across time and cultures, often depicted with wings and halos, symbols of their divine nature and mission. But beyond these traditional images lies a concept that transcends religious confines: angels as pure energy, as messengers of the universe, here to steer us toward our highest good, our utmost potential. Whether you envision them as celestial beings or feel them as a surge of inspired thought, their essence is the same—a force of unconditional love and support.

The presence of angels in our lives need not be an idea shrouded in mystery or fear, for they are believed to be entities of pure benevolence. To some, they are guardians watching over us; to others, they are the intuition that nudges us towards a certain path, the serendipitous help that arrives just in time, or the comforting presence when we are lost in the dark. They are the embodiment of the goodness that the universe holds for each of us, a reminder that we are never alone, that we are always supported by energies greater than we can fully comprehend.

This chapter will explore how we might understand and connect with these gentle forces. We'll look at angels as messengers who bring guidance that can light our way—sometimes in the form of profound realisations, other times as subtle hints or synchronicities that, if heeded, can lead us toward making decisions that resonate deeply with the core of who we are.

We'll also journey through ways to open our hearts and minds to receive this guidance. Just as a radio must be tuned to the right frequency to catch a station, so too must we attune ourselves to the subtle frequencies where angelic guidance resides. From meditation techniques that help quiet the mind to practices that foster a sense of inner peace and receptivity, we'll explore the multitude of pathways that can lead to a profound dialogue with the energies that many call angels.

As we embark on this exploration, let us set aside any preconceived notions and embrace the possibility of a magical, yet very real aspect of existence. Let us open the doors to a more enchanted understanding of our world, where the guidance of angels is but a thought, a whisper, or a feeling away, ready to guide us through life's labyrinth towards the light of our greatest potential. Venturing into the essence of angels requires us to peel back the layers of myth and folklore that have clothed these entities in human-like garb for millennia. At their core, angels are considered to be expressions of divine energy, conduits of the ultimate source, however one might define it. They are thought to exist beyond the physical realm, in a dimension where form as we understand it dissolves into pure presence and intention.

To speak of angels is to speak of an unbounded compassion, a universal benevolence that transcends religious doctrine, cultural constructs, and our limited human perceptions. They are often conceived as messengers—hence the term 'angelos' in ancient Greek, meaning 'messenger'—sent to offer wisdom, comfort, and sometimes to intervene on behalf of the greater good. In countless narratives, they are the bearers of profound revelations, the givers of hope in moments of despair, and the silent guardians who walk alongside us, unseen but deeply felt.

The true nature of angels might be less about their physical depiction and more about their energetic imprint on our lives. It is this energy that speaks to the heart in moments of need, that whispers guidance when we are at a crossroads, and that offers solace when we grieve. Whether one envisions them with wings or perceives them as a palpable, but unseen force, their role remains consistent: they are believed to be entities fully aligned with the highest expressions of love and light, dedicated to supporting the soul's journey towards understanding, purpose, and peace.

When we strip away the traditional imagery and open ourselves to the concept of angels as pure energy, we enter a space where our own inner knowing, our intuition, becomes the medium through which they communicate. Here, an angelic encounter may not be a vision but a sudden surge of inspiration, a coincidental meeting that steers our path in a new direction, or a comforting warmth in times of solitude.

In recognising angels in this energy form, we begin to understand their accessibility. They are not reserved for the saintly or the spiritually elite but are ever-present resource for all. The guidance they offer is not shouted from the heavens but often comes in the quiet moments of reflection, in the sudden clarity after long confusion, or in the inexplicable peace amid turmoil. This understanding of angels allows us to connect with them more freely, seeing their guidance as a natural, integral part of the fabric of our existence.

As we prepare to explore the methods of connecting with this angelic guidance, It is important to approach with an open heart and mind. The connection does not require elaborate rituals or esoteric knowledge but rather a simple, sincere intention to tune in to the higher frequencies where these energies reside. It is about cultivating a state of receptivity, where the mind is quiet enough to hear the subtleties of intuition and the heart is open enough to feel the profound love that angelic presence brings.

In this chapter, as we journey through the concept of angelic guidance, we'll examine not only the traditional roles that angels are believed to play but also the personal stories and experiences that bring these roles to life. We'll look at how the energies we label as 'angels' interact with us, offering protection, insight, and the gentle push we sometimes need to find our way. And for those moments when we are standing at life's precipice, facing the vast unknown, we'll consider how the assurance of angelic support can embolden us to take the leap of faith, trusting that we are guided, loved, and never truly alone.

Archangels

Archangels are believed to be among the highest-ranking angels in the celestial hierarchy, serving as chief messengers and powerful guardians within various spiritual traditions. While there are many interpretations across different cultures and religions, they are generally seen as the bridge between humanity and the divine, embodying universal energies that are potent and expansive. The concept of Archangels is present in several religious texts, including but not limited to, the Bible, the Quran, and other spiritual writings. They are often described as being timeless and, sometimes, as having responsibilities over the natural elements, seasons, or even celestial bodies.

Their roles are to enact the will of the cosmos, to uphold the balance of spiritual laws, and to carry out divine decrees. In the grand context of the universe, Archangels are thought to be responsible for overseeing the collective aspects of human experience. They are not limited to personal guidance but are concerned with the larger themes of human consciousness and global issues. It is believed that each Archangel holds dominion over certain aspects of creation and existence, embodying specific divine attributes, and they can be called upon for assistance in their respective realms.

In essence, Archangels are seen not just as beings but as profound energies that can influence vast areas of life. They are neither male nor female, though they have been assigned genders in various depictions, and they transcend human limitations, existing more as facets of divine energy than individual entities with personal characteristics. The existence and role of Archangels are matters of faith and belief, with personal experiences and anecdotes often serving as the basis for individual understanding. Whether through meditation, prayer, or spiritual practice, many believe that they can connect with these powerful energies, calling upon the guidance and assistance of Archangels to navigate life's complexities.

The enigma of Archangels is as captivating as it is ancient, weaving through the tapestry of human spirituality with threads of mystery and majesty. To speak of Archangels is to delve into a realm where the spiritual meets the cosmic, where the emissaries of the divine operate at a level that encompasses and transcends our individual experiences.

Archangels are often depicted as holding the space where the infinite expanse of the universe touches the personal journey of the soul. They are believed to operate on a vibrational frequency that is higher and more complex than that of guardian angels or other spiritual guides, which allows them to administer to the broad swathes of the human condition and the workings of the cosmos.

In many spiritual narratives, Archangels are entrusted with the stewardship of life's fundamental aspects—such as love, healing, courage, and justice—each Archangel orchestrating their domain with divine precision. They are seen as master architects of fate and destiny, influencing the underlying energy patterns that form the foundation of reality.

Their existence speaks to a shared human longing for connection with a higher power, for intermediaries who can convey our desires and pleas to the divine and bring down wisdom and insight from a realm beyond our ordinary senses. Across cultures, Archangels are the named forces to whom we attribute the miracles of life, the uncanny occurrences that seem to defy explanation, and the moments of transcendence that lift us beyond the ordinary.

The belief in Archangels also brings comfort and a sense of order to the chaos of human life. In times of turmoil and uncertainty, the idea that there are beings of immense power and goodness watching over the collective human experience can be deeply reassuring. Their presence is a balm to the weary soul and a beacon of light in the darkness, offering a glimpse of the celestial order that underpins our worldly existence.

To connect with Archangels, many suggest aligning oneself with the qualities they represent. It is less about invoking them as external agents and more about awakening the corresponding energies within oneself. By meditating on the concepts of harmony, balance, courage, and healing, one is thought to tap into the same reservoir of power that the Archangels draw from, invoking their essence in one's life.

As we prepare to learn more about the roles commonly attributed to specific Archangels, we approach with an openness to the mysteries of the spiritual realm, ready to explore the ways in which these mighty guardians have been understood and revered throughout history and how they continue to inspire those who seek their counsel today.

Archangel Micahel

Archangel Michael, known across many cultures and spiritual traditions, is perhaps the most called upon of the Archangels, renowned for his unwavering courage and his mission to provide protection. His name, resonant with the question "Who is like God?", signifies his embodiment of divine strength and righteousness. Often envisioned brandishing a sword of light, Michael is a symbol of the fight against darkness, a guardian against all that is not in alignment with love and truth.

For those seeking solace and safety in times of trouble, Michael is a beacon of hope. He represents the triumph of light over shadow, a protective presence that many believe can be felt physically as a warm, encompassing energy. His aid is sought not only for personal protection but also for the strength to overcome obstacles, for the bravery to face life's battles, and for help in clearing away fear that hinders spiritual and personal growth.

The colour blue is frequently associated with Michael, mirroring the clarity and tranquillity of a sky unblemished by clouds. It is a colour that represents both the depth of the spiritual realm and the clarity of pure truth. In moments of meditation or prayer, envisioning a blue light can be a method of inviting Michael's presence, symbolizing a shield being woven around you to ward off the negative and uphold the positive.

In seeking Michael's guidance, It is not unusual for individuals to sense a shift in the atmosphere—perhaps a sudden drop in temperature or a comforting breeze—as if to signal his arrival. People often report feeling a greater sense of security and empowerment after calling on him, reflecting his role as a supporter of humanity's inherent strength and divine spark.

To connect with Archangel Michael, you don't need complex rituals; a simple, heartfelt invocation is enough. You might say, "Archangel Michael, please surround me with your protective light," and imagine his presence encircling you. It is believed that he hears all calls for aid, no matter how softly spoken or urgently cried out, and responds with the protective embrace of his wings or the fortifying power of his sword.

As we proceed, each Archangel will reveal their specialties and the ways they offer guidance, but Michael stands out as the protector, a stalwart ally in our quest for safety and inner peace. His is a presence that assures us that we are never battling alone and that within us and beside us, there is a force invincible, ready to lead us through our darkest nights and into the dawn.

Archangel Raphael: The Healing Emissary

In the celestial realm, where Archangels preside with their distinct purposes, Archangel Raphael shines brightly as the beacon of healing and restoration. Raphael, whose name means "God Heals," or "He Who Heals" in Hebrew, is universally recognise d across various spiritual traditions as the supreme healer, not only of physical maladies but also of emotional, mental, and spiritual afflictions. Raphael's healing extends beyond the individual, touching upon the Earth itself and all its inhabitants. This Archangel's emerald, green aura is often visualised in meditations and healing practices, symbolizing the life force that rejuvenates and restores balance. Those who call upon Raphael might seek not just the alleviation of physical symptoms but the healing of the heart and soul, the mending of broken spirits, and the guidance towards peace and wellness.

Traditionally, Raphael is invoked for protection during medical procedures, for the strength to overcome addictions and unhealthy habits, and for the illumination of minds in the quest for medical knowledge and discovery. Medical professionals, caregivers, and those suffering from health issues might find solace and support in Raphael's loving presence, seeking his assistance in their journey towards healing. Beyond the physical, Raphael's domain encompasses the emotional and spiritual realms. He aids in the healing of emotional wounds, helping to release buried traumas and to cleanse the heart of resentments and fears. His guidance is sought in the pursuit of inner peace, self-forgiveness, and the transformation of negative energies into positive growth. For those walking the path of spiritual awakening, Raphael serves as a compassionate guide, illuminating the journey with his healing light. He supports the clearing of spiritual blockages, facilitating a deeper connection with the divine and a greater understanding of one's spiritual purpose.

Engaging with Raphael's energy involves an openness to receive healing in all its forms. You might visualise a soothing, green light enveloping you, penetrating deeply into areas of physical or emotional pain, dissolving them with its radiance. Prayers, affirmations, and meditations focused on healing can serve as powerful conduits for Raphael's restorative energies. An invocation to Raphael need not be elaborate. A simple heartfelt request, such as, "Archangel Raphael, please surround me with your healing light," can suffice to draw his presence nearby. Trust in Raphael's ability to guide the process of healing, often in ways that may differ from your expectations but that ultimately lead to the highest good.

Those attuned to Raphael's guidance often report experiencing signs or synchronicities that affirm his healing presence. These can include sudden insights related to health, serendipitous encounters with healers or therapeutic modalities, or the appearance of green lights or orbs. Such occurrences are Raphael's way of signalling his active involvement in your healing journey. Raphael's work is not confined to individual healing alone. He also oversees environmental and planetary well-being, encouraging humans to live in harmony with nature and to take actions that support the Earth's health. In this capacity,

Raphael inspires ecological initiatives, conservation efforts, and a deeper respect for the natural world.

Countless individuals have shared stories of profound healings attributed to Raphael's intervention—miraculous recoveries, unexpected improvements in chronic conditions, and significant life changes stemming from emotional and spiritual healings. These testimonies underscore the profound impact of Raphael's presence, offering hope and validation for those who seek his aid.

In embracing Archangel Raphael's presence in our lives, we open ourselves to a multifaceted healing journey that transcends the physical. Raphael invites us to view healing as a holistic process that encompasses our entire being—body, mind, and spirit—and extends outward to the world around us. By fostering a relationship with this powerful emissary of healing, we not only invite restoration and balance into our lives but also contribute to the greater healing of our planet. In the presence of Raphael, we are reminded that no wound is too deep, no ailment too stubborn, and no heartache too profound to be beyond the reach of divine healing. With each step taken in faith towards recovery and wholeness, Archangel Raphael walks beside us, guiding, healing, and illuminating the path with his emerald light.

Archangel Gabriel

In the celestial choir of Archangels, another luminous figure stands out for their profound role in the human experience: Archangel Gabriel. Known as the messenger of God, Gabriel's essence is interwoven with the themes of communication, revelation, and inspiration. Holding a trumpet or a lily, Gabriel is often depicted as the herald of divine messages, the bringer of good news, and the guide for those seeking clarity and purpose in their lives.

Gabriel's presence in spiritual texts is marked by significant announcements that carry deep spiritual importance. From heralding the birth of John the Baptist to announcing to Mary the birth of Jesus, Gabriel's messages have been pivotal in shaping the course of spiritual history. This legacy of divine communication positions Gabriel not just as a conveyor of news but as a bridge between the divine will and human understanding, offering insight and clarity to those who seek guidance on their path.

The Archangel Gabriel is especially revered by writers, artists, journalists, and communicators, serving as a patron of creative expression and clear articulation. Gabriel's guidance is sought for inspiration, for the courage to speak one's truth, and for assistance in connecting deeply with others through words and art. In moments of creative block or when words fail to capture the depth of one's thoughts and emotions, invoking Gabriel's presence can open the floodgates of inspiration, allowing divine creativity to flow freely.

Connecting with Gabriel often involves creating space for silence and listening, for it is in the quiet moments that we are most receptive to the subtle whispers of guidance. Those who work with Gabriel sometimes choose to write letters expressing their deepest questions and desires, leaving them in a sacred space as an invitation for divine insight. Others might meditate with the intention of opening their heart and mind to receive Gabriel's wisdom, visualizing the Archangel's light illuminating their path to understanding and expression.

Gabriel's influence extends beyond the realm of personal creativity, touching all areas of communication and understanding. This Archangel aids in overcoming fears and insecurities related to self-expression, empowering individuals to share their inner truth with confidence and grace. Whether it is navigating difficult conversations, expressing one's needs and desires, or sharing one's soul's work with the world, Gabriel stands ready to lend strength and support.

In today's fast-paced world, where misunderstandings and miscommunications are commonplace, Gabriel's role as a facilitator of clear, heartfelt communication is more important than ever. The Archangel encourages us to listen not only with our ears but with our hearts, fostering empathy and deeper connections among people.

For those embarking on new beginnings, be it in their personal lives, careers, or spiritual journeys, Gabriel is a beacon of hope and renewal. Just as this Archangel announced the coming of transformative forces in sacred texts, so too can Gabriel herald the start of new chapters in our lives, guiding us through transitions with a sense of purpose and direction.

In engaging with Gabriel's energy, we are reminded of the power of our words and thoughts, the importance of listening to our inner voice, and the transformative potential of communicating with authenticity and integrity. Gabriel's guidance inspires us to live our truth, to share our unique light with the world, and to remain open to the endless possibilities that unfold when we align our voice with the divine.

As we continue to explore the manifold ways in which the Archangels influence and enrich our lives, the presence of Gabriel stands as a testament to the beauty and power of divine communication. In a universe where every soul has a story to tell, Gabriel's guidance ensures that our narratives are heard, understood, and cherished, weaving the fabric of human connection with threads of truth, love, and clarity.

Archangel Uriel

Transitioning from the luminous guidance of Gabriel, we encounter the gentle, nurturing presence of Archangel Uriel, whose name means "Light of God." Uriel's domain encompasses wisdom, enlightenment, and the transmutation of lower energies into higher understanding. Unlike the other archangels who serve more explicit roles such as protection, healing, and communication, Uriel's essence is steeped in the quiet glow of wisdom, offering insight and illumination to those wandering in the darkness of confusion or seeking the light of truth.

Uriel is often depicted holding a flame or a lantern, symbolizing the light of knowledge that dispels ignorance and fear. This archangel is considered a patron of the arts and sciences, guiding scholars, educators, and seekers of truth down the path of intellectual and spiritual discovery. Uriel's flame not only lights the way but also purifies, transforming misunderstanding and doubt into clarity and conviction.

Invoking Uriel's guidance is particularly powerful during times of decision-making or when faced with challenging situations that require not just knowledge, but deep wisdom. Uriel assists in illuminating the choices before us, ensuring that our decisions are aligned with our highest good and the greater harmony of all involved. This archangel's energy supports the process of turning knowledge into wisdom, guiding us to apply our learnings in ways that enrich our lives and the world around us.

To connect with Uriel, one might meditate on the flame of truth, visualizing it burning away all that obscures our highest path. Some find solace in walking in nature, where the light of the sun and the stars speaks of Uriel's omnipresent glow, reminding us that divine wisdom permeates every corner of the universe. It is in these moments of quiet reflection that Uriel's whispers can be heard most clearly, offering insights that resonate with the soul's deepest yearnings for understanding.

Uriel also plays a crucial role in times of natural disaster or global crisis. This archangel is called upon for help in stabilizing situations, bringing calm where there is chaos, and offering solutions that restore balance and peace. Uriel's presence reminds us that even in the midst of turmoil, there is an underlying order and logic, a universal wisdom that guides us towards resolution and healing.

For those exploring the depths of their own consciousness, Uriel is a beacon of inner light, illuminating the shadows within and revealing the gifts that lie hidden in our deepest selves. This archangel encourages us to look within for answers, to trust the wisdom of our higher selves, and to see challenges as opportunities for growth and transformation.

In engaging with Uriel, we are invited to rise above the mundane, to see our lives and our choices from a higher perspective. Uriel teaches that true wisdom comes from a place of compassion, humility, and a profound connection to the divine spark within us all. This archangel's guidance empowers us to become beacons of light in our own right, illuminating the path for others with our actions, our words, and our very being.

As we journey through the realm of the Archangels, Uriel's presence enriches our understanding of the multifaceted ways in which divine guidance manifests. In the pursuit of knowledge, in the quest for peace, and in the depths of introspection, Uriel stands as a testament to the transformative power of wisdom, reminding us that every moment of uncertainty is also an opportunity for enlightenment and growth.

Archangel Chamuel

After the illuminating wisdom of Uriel, we are drawn to the compassionate embrace of Archangel Chamuel, whose name is often interpreted as "One Who Seeks God" or "He Who Sees God." Chamuel's realm is that of pure love and peaceful relationships, guiding souls towards harmonious connections and inner peace. This archangel's energy is a gentle, pink light, enveloping all in warmth and affection, encouraging the opening of the heart to give and receive love in its most unconditional form.

Chamuel is the seeker of the lost, not only in the physical sense but also in helping individuals find peace, purpose, and a place within the universal tapestry of love. This archangel aids in mending broken relationships, soothing troubled hearts, and guiding us to see the love that binds us all together. Chamuel's mission is deeply intertwined with the quest for personal and global peace, making this archangel a beacon for those working to resolve conflict and foster understanding among people.

Invoking Chamuel's assistance can be particularly powerful when navigating the complexities of personal dynamics, whether seeking to heal rifts in family relationships, wishing to deepen connections with friends, or longing for a soulmate. Chamuel's guidance can gently steer us towards recognising the love that is already present in our lives, opening our eyes to the connections that sustain and enrich us.

To connect with Archangel Chamuel, one might visualise a soft, pink light—representative of unconditional love—surrounding and permeating their being. This visualization can be accompanied by affirmations of openness to love in all its forms, and a willingness to forgive, heal, and move forward in peace. Chamuel's presence encourages an attitude of gratitude for love's many expressions, reminding us that every act of kindness, every moment of compassion, is a reflection of the divine love that Chamuel embodies.

In moments of loneliness or despair, Chamuel offers a reminder that we are never truly alone, that the love we seek is also seeking us. This archangel's influence extends beyond romantic love to include the love we share in communities, the love we express through creativity and service, and the love we cultivate for ourselves. Chamuel's gentle nudging can help us dismantle the walls we have built around our hearts, allowing the light of love to heal old wounds and illuminate our connections with others.

Beyond the personal, Chamuel's vision of love encompasses the planet, encouraging humanity to transcend differences and unite in a shared commitment to peace and goodwill. This archangel's energy supports peacekeepers, healers, and all who strive to create a world where love prevails over discord, where kindness is the currency that binds us.

In engaging with Chamuel, we are invited to explore the depths of our hearts, to rediscover the joy of loving and being loved, and to envision a world transformed by the healing power of love. Chamuel teaches that the journey to peace, both within and without, begins with a single step taken in love—a step that draws us closer to the divine and to one another, in a dance of harmony that echoes through the ages.

As we continue to explore the celestial guardianship of the Archangels, Chamuel's essence of love serves as a guiding light, reminding us of the transformative power of love and the endless possibilities that unfold when we open our hearts to give and receive the most divine of all gifts.

Archangel Jophiel

Venturing further into the celestial realms, we encounter the serene presence of Archangel Jophiel, known as the "Beauty of God." Jophiel's luminous aura is imbued with the mission to infuse our lives with beauty, appreciation, and optimism. This Archangel encourages us to slow down, to notice the splendor in the world around us, and to cultivate a mindset that sees the beauty in all things. Jophiel's influence extends beyond the visual and aesthetic; it touches upon the beauty of thought, the grace of a well-lived life, and the inner glow that comes from a soul in harmony with itself and the universe.

Jophiel's energy is often associated with the color yellow, a vibrant hue that captures the archangel's essence of illumination and joy. This radiant energy inspires creativity, enlightens the mind, and helps dispel the darkness of negativity and pessimism. In moments when the world seems grey and devoid of colour, Jophiel's presence can reawaken our sense of wonder, reminding us of the endless beauty that life offers to those willing to see it.

Seeking Jophiel's guidance can be particularly meaningful for those pursuing creative endeavours. Artists, writers, and all who create turn to Jophiel for inspiration, for the archangel's touch can transform the mundane into the extraordinary, revealing the magic that lies in the act of creation. But Jophiel's domain is not limited to the traditionally creative; this archangel also aids in seeing the beauty in life's challenges, helping us approach our trials with grace and find the hidden blessings in adversity.

To connect with Archangel Jophiel, one might engage in meditation focused on gratitude for the beauty in their life. Visualizing Jophiel's yellow light can help illuminate the mind's eye, bringing into focus the abundance of beauty that surrounds us, often unnoticed. Creating spaces of beauty in our homes, tending to gardens, or simply committing to notice something beautiful every day are all practices that align us with Jophiel's energy.

Jophiel also serves as a gentle reminder that beauty starts from within, that a peaceful mind and a loving heart reflect the most profound beauty. In times of turmoil or self-doubt, invoking Jophiel can help shift our perspective, guiding us to find balance and beauty in our inner world, which in turn radiates outward.

Moreover, Jophiel's influence encourages us to cultivate an environment that supports our well-being and growth. By clearing clutter and creating spaces that reflect our inner beauty, we invite Jophiel's essence into our lives, enhancing our capacity for joy and creative expression. This archangel's guidance teaches us that beauty is not a superficial adornment but a fundamental aspect of our spiritual path, enriching our journey and elevating our soul.

As we traverse the landscape of our lives, Jophiel stands as a beacon of light, encouraging us to appreciate the present moment, to revel in the act of creation, and to remember that, even in the most ordinary settings, the extraordinary can be found. In the cultivation of beauty, both within our hearts and in the world around us, we find a path to transcendence, guided by Jophiel's vision of a world where every soul shines brightly, reflecting the divine beauty from which we all stem.

Archangel Zadkiel

As we continue our celestial journey, we are embraced by the tranquil presence of Archangel Zadkiel, often known as the "Righteousness of God." Zadkiel's realm is one of forgiveness, mercy, and transmutation, providing the divine assistance necessary to release old pains, forgive ourselves and others, and transform negative energies into positive growth. This Archangel embodies the violet flame, a spiritual energy that purifies and heals emotional scars, allowing us to move forward with freedom and clarity.

Zadkiel's guidance is sought not just in moments of personal reflection and atonement but also in the broader context of learning and memory enhancement. Often associated with the color violet, Zadkiel aids students and learners of all ages in retaining information and overcoming obstacles to understanding. This archangel's gentle yet powerful influence can open the mind, making the acquisition of knowledge and the journey of intellectual exploration both fruitful and enjoyable.

In the practice of forgiveness, Zadkiel serves as a compassionate guide, helping us navigate the often difficult process of letting go of resentment and anger. The act of forgiveness, as encouraged by Zadkiel, is not about condoning hurtful actions but about liberating oneself from the chains of past grievances. This liberation is seen as a pathway to spiritual growth, creating space in our hearts and minds for love and light to enter.

To invite Archangel Zadkiel's presence into your life, consider engaging in meditations focused on the violet flame. Visualise this purifying energy enveloping you, burning away negativity, and filling your being with a sense of peace and renewal. Affirmations of forgiveness and self-compassion can also be powerful tools in aligning with Zadkiel's vibration, reinforcing the intention to heal and move beyond past hurts.

Zadkiel also encourages the practice of gratitude as a means to elevate one's vibrational energy. By focusing on the blessings in our lives, we initiate a positive feedback loop that attracts more of what we are grateful for, further empowering us to transmute challenges into opportunities for growth.

Furthermore, Zadkiel's influence extends to those seeking to make positive changes in their lives. Whether It is transforming a habit, altering a life path, or adopting a more spiritual outlook, Zadkiel offers the encouragement and support necessary for such transitions. This archangel's energy reminds us that change is not only possible but is a natural part of the soul's evolution towards its highest potential.

In the tapestry of Archangelic guidance, Zadkiel's thread is one of profound transformation and healing. Through forgiveness, we find the strength to release the past; through learning, we embrace the future; and through transmutation, we discover the alchemy of the spirit, capable of turning the lead of our experiences into the gold of wisdom and understanding. Zadkiel's presence in our lives is a testament to the power of grace, urging us to rise above our limitations and to soar towards the limitless possibilities of growth and enlightenment.

ArchAngel Sandalphon

Embarking further on our exploration of the celestial guardians, we are greeted by the soothing presence of Archangel Sandalphon, often regarded as the twin brother of Archangel Metatron. Sandalphon's unique role within the archangelic realm is as the messenger who delivers prayers from Earth to the Divine, acting as a bridge between humanity and the celestial. Known for his connection to music and poetry, Sandalphon inspires those who seek to express the deepest desires of their hearts and souls through artistic endeavours.

Sandalphon is associated with grounding and connection to the Earth, reminding us of the importance of our physical journey alongside our spiritual one. This Archangel encourages us to find harmony and balance in our lives, integrating the spiritual with the mundane, ensuring that our feet are firmly planted even as we reach for the divine. The presence of Sandalphon can be especially comforting during times of isolation or disconnection, offering a reminder that our prayers, hopes, and dreams are heard and valued.

Engaging with Sandalphon may involve music as a medium for spiritual communication and expression. It is believed that by singing, playing musical instruments, or even simply listening to music that touches the soul, we can facilitate a closer connection with this Archangel. Sandalphon's energy amplifies the healing and transformative power of music, allowing it to open hearts, heal wounds, and elevate the spirit.

To invite Sandalphon's guidance into your life, consider creating a sacred space where you can express your prayers or desires through writing, music, or art. Visualization practices that focus on grounding and the nurturing energy of the Earth can also help attune you to Sandalphon's vibration. Imagine sending your prayers and intentions upward, through the layers of the cosmos, with Sandalphon acting as the guardian who ensures they reach their divine destination.

Sandalphon also plays a pivotal role in helping us appreciate the beauty and significance of the present moment. By encouraging us to live fully in the here and now, this Archangel aids in the realisation that heaven is not a distant realm, but a state that can be experienced in the everyday. Sandalphon's presence teaches us that each moment, each breath, is a prayer in itself, and that our most profound spiritual experiences often arise from the simplest acts of living.

Furthermore, Sandalphon's influence is said to extend to environmental stewardship, urging us to care for our planet as a sacred trust. This Archangel inspires us to act in ways that honour the Earth, reminding us of our responsibility to preserve and protect the natural world for future generations.

In the rich mosaic of archangelic guidance, Sandalphon stands out as the guardian of expression and the sacredness of the earthly journey. Through music, art, and prayer, Sandalphon helps us weave the fabric of our dreams into the tapestry of reality, grounding our spiritual aspirations in the beauty of the physical world. As we journey with Sandalphon, we are reminded that our prayers are a powerful force for change, capable of transcending the boundaries between Earth and the divine, and that in the act of creation, we touch the face of the infinite.

Arch Angel Raziel

As we continue to navigate the celestial realms, we encounter Archangel Raziel, often known as the "Keeper of Secrets" and the "Angel of Mysteries." Raziel stands as a profound figure within the archangelic hierarchy, holding the keys to divine wisdom, esoteric knowledge, and the understanding of the universe's deeper truths. This archangel is said to have written the "Book of Raziel," a compendium of heavenly secrets, mystical knowledge, and a guide to understanding both the physical and spiritual worlds.

Raziel's essence is that of illumination, bringing light to the shadows of our ignorance and fear, and revealing the interconnectedness of all things. He invites us into the depths of our own souls, encouraging exploration of the mysteries that lie within. Raziel's guidance is sought by those who wish to delve deeper into spiritual practices, to unlock the secrets of the universe, and to gain insight into the workings of the cosmos and their place within it.

The presence of Raziel can be particularly impactful for spiritual seekers, mystics, and those engaged in esoteric studies. This Archangel assists in deciphering the symbolic language of the universe, aiding in the interpretation of dreams, visions, and intuitive insights. Raziel encourages us to look beyond the surface, to question and seek understanding, and to embrace the journey of discovery with an open heart and mind.

Connecting with Archangel Raziel involves a willingness to step into the unknown, to trust in the journey of enlightenment, and to be open to receiving wisdom in various forms. Meditation and study are pathways to accessing Raziel's guidance, as is the practice of journaling one's insights, dreams, and experiences. Visualizing Raziel's indigo light can help open the third eye chakra, the centre of intuition and insight, facilitating a deeper connection to the angelic realms and the higher self.

Raziel's influence extends to creativity, inspiring artists, writers, and inventors to tap into the universal flow of ideas and to bring forth innovations that reflect the divine spark of creation. By encouraging us to harness our creative potential, Raziel helps us to manifest our visions and dreams into reality, showing us that we are co-creators in the unfolding story of the universe.

For those who seek understanding of life's deeper mysteries, Raziel offers guidance and support, reminding us that true wisdom comes from within. This Archangel teaches that each soul carries a spark of the divine, and that by seeking knowledge and understanding, we not only illuminate our own paths but also contribute to the collective enlightenment of humanity.

In the rich tapestry of archangelic guidance, Raziel's thread is one of profound mystery and enlightenment, weaving through the fabric of our lives the reminder that the universe is a place of endless wonder and infinite possibility. As we journey with Raziel, we are encouraged to embrace our curiosity, to explore the depths of our spiritual heritage, and to uncover the sacred truths that lie waiting in the silence of our being. Through this exploration, we discover not only the mysteries of the cosmos but also the boundless potential of our own souls.

Archangel Haniel

Our celestial journey now brings us to the tranquil presence of Archangel Haniel, often associated with the grace and harmony of the divine feminine. Haniel, whose name can be translated as "Glory of God" or "Grace of God," embodies the nurturing aspects of the universe, offering support in fostering beauty, intuition, and emotional balance. This archangel's essence is like the gentle glow of moonlight, soothing and serene, illuminating our path with a soft, compassionate light.

Haniel is closely connected to the moon and its cycles, reflecting the archangel's role in helping us navigate the ebbs and flows of our emotional landscapes. Just as the moon influences the tides, Haniel aids in the mastery of our feelings, encouraging us to embrace our emotional depth and sensitivity as a source of strength. This guidance is especially powerful for those seeking to deepen their connection with their intuition, to harness their innate psychic abilities, or to cultivate a more harmonious relationship with themselves and others.

Engaging with Haniel's energy can bring a sense of peace and centeredness, reminding us of the beauty in simplicity and the power of grace in action. To connect with this archangel, one might seek quiet moments under the night sky, allowing the moon's luminescence to serve as a conduit for Haniel's gentle guidance. Meditation focused on the heart chakra, envisioning a radiant light filling and healing the space, can also help attune to Haniel's vibration, opening the heart to give and receive love freely and fully.

Haniel encourages us to honour our natural cycles of activity and rest, of giving and receiving, teaching us to find balance in our lives. This archangel's support is invaluable in times of transition, offering guidance on embracing change with grace and finding the hidden blessings in the challenges we face. Haniel's presence is a reminder that true strength lies in vulnerability, in the willingness to be open and receptive to life's myriad experiences.

For those involved in healing professions or spiritual practices, Haniel can be a profound ally, deepening the practitioner's ability to connect with divine energy and to facilitate healing for themselves and others. This archangel's influence inspires creativity, beauty, and artistry, encouraging us to express our innermost feelings and to share our unique gifts with the world.

Haniel also plays a crucial role in helping us to cultivate self-love and acceptance, guiding us to see ourselves through the eyes of the divine, as beings of light and beauty. By fostering a deep appreciation for our own worth, Haniel empowers us to step into our power, to live authentically, and to radiate our inner grace outward, touching the lives of others with our presence.

In the celestial chorus, Haniel's melody is one of sublime beauty and profound emotional wisdom, inviting us to dance to the rhythm of our hearts and to live in harmony with the universe. Through Haniel's guidance, we learn that grace is not merely an attribute but a way of being, a path that leads us to discover the divine within and around us, in every moment and every breath.

Archangel Ariel

Concluding our celestial odyssey, we turn our gaze towards Archangel Ariel, whose name signifies "Lioness of God." Ariel is often associated with the natural world, environmentalism, and the protection of animals. This archangel's essence is interwoven with the Earth's vitality, safeguarding its ecosystems and guiding those who seek to preserve the beauty and balance of the natural environment. Ariel's presence is a reminder of our deep connection to the planet, urging us to live in harmony with nature and to honour our role as stewards of the Earth.

Ariel is believed to oversee the elemental world, working closely with the spirits of nature to maintain the health and well-being of our planet. This includes not only wild spaces but urban environments as well, reminding us that the divine can be found in all corners of the Earth. Ariel's energy encourages us to appreciate the abundance and fertility of the land, to understand the intricate web of life in which we play a part, and to act with compassion and mindfulness towards all beings.

Connecting with Archangel Ariel can be as simple as stepping outside and allowing yourself to be fully present in the natural world. Whether It is a walk in the park, tending to a garden, or simply observing the birds from a window, these acts of connection can serve as a bridge to Ariel's guidance. For those seeking to deepen their relationship with this archangel, environmental activism, conservation efforts, and practices that reduce one's ecological footprint can align closely with Ariel's mission.

Ariel's protective energy also extends to individual endeavours, particularly those that require courage, focus, and determination. This archangel empowers us to pursue our passions and to overcome obstacles, providing the strength and support needed to achieve our goals. Ariel inspires a sense of adventure and exploration, urging us to discover the magic hidden in the world around us and to embrace the journey of life with a brave heart.

For those drawn to the healing arts, Ariel offers insight into the healing properties of plants and natural remedies, deepening our understanding of herbal medicine and the Earth's healing gifts. This archangel encourages holistic approaches to health and wellness, emphasizing the connection between the health of our bodies and the health of our planet.

In meditation or prayer, envisioning Ariel surrounded by a soft, earthy green light can help attune to this archangel's energy, reinforcing our bond with nature and awakening an awareness of the sacredness of life in all its forms. Ariel's guidance teaches us that every action, no matter how small, can contribute to the well-being of the

Earth, encouraging us to live with intention and reverence for the natural world.

As we conclude our journey through the realm of the Archangels, Ariel's message of environmental stewardship and respect for all life forms serves as a powerful reminder of our interconnectedness with the Earth and the divine. Through Ariel's guidance, we are invited to witness the wonder of creation, to protect and cherish the planet that sustains us, and to walk gently upon it, leaving a trail of harmony and hope for future generations. In the embrace of Ariel, we find the courage to act on behalf of the Earth, embodying the change we wish to see in the world and living each day as a testament to the beauty and resilience of the natural world.

****

While the cosmos is graced with a multitude of Archangels, each offering their unique brand of celestial guidance, the insights shared thus far aim to illuminate your understanding of these heavenly beings. If you had approached me years ago with tales of communing with angels, I would have recoiled, perhaps even laughed. The very notion of invisible entities existing beyond our perceptual boundaries was enough to unsettle me. Yet, life has a way of unveiling the unseen, of guiding us to truths beyond our initial comprehension. Through personal encounters and the subtle yet unmistakable signs of their presence, I have come to not only believe in the guidance of these celestial guardians but to rely on their protection and wisdom. The reality that unfolds before our eyes is but a fraction of what truly exists.

It is not necessary to envisage these beings as winged messengers adrift in the heavens; what's essential is the recognition of their presence. Our human minds are adept at painting pictures, yet the feelings we experience, the sense of another's presence—that is something far more profound. In moments of meditation, when the chatter of the mind quiets, a realisation dawns: we are surrounded, embraced by a presence that is both ancient and infinitely caring. Engaging with this presence, seeking its guidance, and observing the signs it bestows, one begins to perceive the world anew.

My own journey into the realm of angelic guidance began somewhat unexpectedly, with Boni Lonnsburry's "The Map" serving as my introduction. I recall a winter morning, walking my dog Nayla around 5.30AM, listening to the audiobook. Initially, the concepts presented stirred a sense of unease within me. However, propelled by a blend of curiosity and scepticism, I silently requested a sign, a confirmation of the angels' reality. After few minutes as I carried on walking, there was not just the sudden, serene descent of snowflakes but an overwhelming sense of peace, a tranquillity so profound that it felt me with complete amazement. It was in this moment that my belief took root, nurtured by the undeniable sense of calm and the magic woven into that winter morning.

Over the years, this belief has only deepened. In times of worry for my daughter's health even if it is just a minor cold, I have reached out to Archangel Raphael for his protective embrace. When concerns for my pets arise, I turn to Archangel Ariel. Each plea for guidance, every whispered prayer for assistance, has been met with signs and wonders that affirm their vigilant presence in my life.

This journey has taught me that the angelic realm is not so much about celestial beings adorned with halos and wings but about the profound connections and guidance available to us. It is a testament to the unseen forces that guide, protect, and enrich our lives, inviting us to explore the vastness of our existence and to embrace the mystery with an open heart. In sharing these experiences, I hope to bridge the gap between doubt and belief, between the seen and the unseen, encouraging you to seek your own encounters with the divine presence that surrounds us all.

Below you can find two different methods to connecting to the archangels, this should be a good starting point to start your journey.

"The Embrace": A Guided Meditation for Connection

"The Embrace" is a gentle, guided meditation designed to foster a serene connection with the Archangelic realm, allowing you to experience their guidance and support in a comforting and non-intimidating way. This meditation can be practiced anywhere you feel at peace—within your home, in nature, or any space where you can be undisturbed for a few moments.

Preparation

- Find a quiet, comfortable place where you can sit or lie down without interruptions.
- You may choose to light a candle or incense to create a tranquil atmosphere, but It is not necessary.
- Have an open heart and mind.

Meditation Steps

- Close your eyes and take several deep breaths. With each inhale, feel calmness washing over you. With each exhale, release any tension in your body. Continue this breathing pattern until you feel relaxed and cantered.
- Imagine a soft, radiant sphere of light hovering above you. This light can be any colour that you associate with peace and

safety. As you focus on this sphere, it begins to gently descend, enveloping you in a warm, comforting glow.

- Silently, or in a whisper, invite the Archangels to join you in this sacred space. You don't need to call them by name; simply express your openness to their presence and guidance. Trust that they are with you, offering their support and love.

- As you sit within this sphere of light, feel the presence of the Archangels surrounding you. Imagine their energy as a gentle embrace, uplifting and protecting you. Allow yourself to receive their love, to feel their guidance flowing into your heart and mind.

- In this space of connection, let your heart be open to any messages, feelings, or insights that come to you. The guidance from the Archangels may be subtle—a sensation, a whisper of intuition, a sudden understanding or clarity about a situation in your life. Trust what you receive, knowing it is given with unconditional love.

- Whether you have received clear guidance or simply enjoyed a few moments of peace, take a moment to express your gratitude to the Archangels for their presence and support. Gratitude deepens our connection to the divine and opens our hearts to further guidance.

- Gently bring your awareness back to your surroundings. Wiggle your fingers and toes, stretch if you need to, and when you are ready, open your eyes. Carry the peace and any guidance you have received with you as you continue your day.

"The Embrace" meditation can be revisited anytime you seek guidance, comfort, or simply a moment of peace. It is a reminder that you are never alone, that celestial support is always available, inviting you into a deeper understanding of the universe and your place within it.

The Angelic Beacon: Recognising Signs and Connecting with Guidance

Preparation

- Find a quiet, comfortable spot where you can relax without interruptions.
- Have a notebook and pen handy for reflections or insights you might want to record afterward.

Steps

- Begin by sitting comfortably, closing your eyes, and focusing on your breath. Take deep, slow breaths to relax your body and calm your mind. With each exhale, release any tension you are holding.

Intention Setting

- Silently, or aloud, set your intention for this practice. It could be as simple as, "I am open to receiving guidance from the Archangels" or "I seek to notice and understand the signs the Archangels send me." Setting a clear intention helps to direct your focus and energy towards connecting with the angelic realm.

- Imagine yourself surrounded by a gentle, glowing light. This light represents the protective and loving energy of the Archangels. Visualise it enveloping you in warmth and safety, creating a sacred space for your meditation.

- Within this space, allow yourself to feel the presence of the Archangels. You might imagine a sense of warmth, a gentle breeze, or simply an overwhelming feeling of love and peace.

- In this state of relaxed awareness, ask the Archangels to send you a sign. This sign can be anything that will resonate with you personally – a specific symbol, a word, a feeling, or even a spontaneous insight.

- Let go of any expectations about what this sign should be or when it will appear. Trust that the Archangels will provide guidance in the way that's best for you.

Gratitude and Closing

- Whether you feel you have received a sign or not, express your gratitude to the Archangels for their presence and support. Gratitude opens the heart and reinforces your connection to the divine.
- Gently bring your awareness back to your surroundings. When you are ready, open your eyes, and if you feel inclined, jot down any experiences, feelings, or signs you received during your meditation in your notebook.

Reflection and Integration

- After "The Angelic Beacon" meditation, spend some time reflecting on any signs or feelings you experienced. Remember, signs from the Archangels can be subtle and may not always be immediate. Stay alert in the days following your meditation; you might notice symbols, words, or situations that resonate with the guidance you sought. The key is to maintain an open heart and mind, allowing the Archangels' guidance to unfold in its own time and way.

This method provides a serene and personal way to foster your connection with the Archangels, inviting their wisdom into your life through mindfulness and the gentle observation of signs.

****

Embracing the presence of the Archangels in your life is an invitation to explore beyond the visible, to engage with forces of compassion, wisdom, and strength that transcend our earthly experiences. Whether through meditation, observing signs, or simply holding space for their presence, connecting with the Archangels can enrich your spiritual journey with layers of meaning and guidance previously unimagined. It is natural to approach this unseen realm with a mix of curiosity and caution. Scepticism is a part of our human nature, guiding us to question and seek proof before fully committing our belief. However, the realm of the Archangels, much like the vastness of love or the depth of intuition, is not always subject to the tangible evidence our minds might crave. It thrives in the space of openness, of willingness to believe that there is more to our existence than what meets the eye.

For those of you hesitant to embark on this journey, remember that connecting with the Archangels does not require a leap of blind faith but rather a step of open-hearted curiosity. Start small—perhaps with a simple acknowledgment of their presence, a quiet request for a sign, or even a meditation focused on the qualities you seek to embody. Pay attention to the subtle shifts in your surroundings, the unexpected coincidences, and the gentle nudges towards growth and healing. These are the whispers of guidance, the fingerprints of the Archangels in your life. Seeking connection with the Archangels is a deeply personal endeavour, one that can unfold in myriad ways. Be patient with yourself and the process and remain open to the possibility of surprise. The guidance you receive may not always take the form you anticipate, but it will come to you in the way that you most need, at the time when you are ready to receive it. In your moments of doubt, remember that the journey is as important as the destination. The act of reaching out, of seeking guidance from the Archangels, is in itself a powerful affirmation of your openness to the divine, your willingness to explore the unseen, and your courage to ask for assistance. Whether you find yourself enveloped in their comforting presence, guided by their unseen hand, or inspired by their whispered wisdom, know that the Archangels are companions on your journey, offering their support, love, and guidance every step of the way.

Let this guidance serve as the beginning of your exploration, a gateway to discovering the profound companionship and guidance that the Archangels can offer. With an open heart and a curious spirit, you are well-equipped to embark on this celestial journey, ready to embrace the wonders and insights that await you in the loving embrace of the Archangels.

Chapter 4: Letting Go Of Control

In our journey through life, the allure of control whispers promises of certainty and safety. It seduces us with the notion that through meticulous planning and unwavering diligence, we can sculpt our future into the masterpiece we envision. The entrepreneur pouring over market analyses and strategic plans embodies this pursuit, driven by the conviction that the right combination of foresight and action can safeguard against failure. Similarly, the parent, diligently curating every aspect of their child's life, operates under the belief that through their vigilance, they can shield their offspring from life's harsher realities and pave a smooth path toward success. These narratives, reflective of a deep-seated human desire to steer the ship of fate, reveal our profound yearning for predictability in a world that dances to the rhythm of **chance and change.** However, life's essence is its fluidity, its capacity to surprise and challenge us, often rendering our best-laid plans obsolete. The entrepreneur wakes to a market in upheaval, where technological advancements or shifts in consumer behaviour cast aside months of planning. The parent, despite their best efforts, finds that their child struggles, not from a lack of care or preparation, but from the natural trials that sculpt character and resilience.

Such moments, while fraught with disappointment and disillusionment, serve as crucial junctures in our spiritual and emotional evolution. They invite us to confront the illusion of control—that while we may influence our journey, we cannot dictate every twist and turn. This realisation, though unsettling, opens the door to profound liberation and growth. It challenges us to release our grip on the reins of life and to trust in the journey, recognising that the beauty of our existence lies not in the certainty of our destination but in the richness of our travel.

This dance with control and its release is not a call to passivity but an invitation to engage with life from a place of trust and openness. It beckons us to participate fully, exerting our will and making our choices, while also accepting that the outcome may differ from our expectations. This balance between action and acceptance is where true growth occurs, where we learn to flow with life's currents rather than against them. Embracing this shift in perspective, where action is balanced with acceptance, cultivates a profound sense of peace and resilience within us. It is akin to a sailor who sets the sails and steers the rudder with skill and intention, yet acknowledges the wind's ultimate command over the journey. This sailor, while adept and prepared, understands that the sea's changing moods and the wind's whims are beyond control. Similarly, as we navigate the vast ocean of life, our efforts are necessary and impactful, but the recognition that some outcomes lie beyond our grasp teaches us humility and fosters a deeper connection with the flow of existence. This delicate balance between effort and surrender does not negate the value of planning or diminish the importance of diligence. Instead, it enriches these endeavours with the wisdom that our true power lies in adaptability, in our capacity to meet unexpected turns with grace and creativity. By holding our plans lightly, ready to adapt and adjust, we become like water—powerful in our softness, capable of carving canyons over time through persistence and flexibility. Letting go invites us into a deeper dialogue with our inner selves. It challenges us to examine the fears that drive our need for control—the fear of failure, of uncertainty, of vulnerability. By confronting these fears, we begin to disentangle our sense of self-worth from the outcomes we achieve, learning instead to value ourselves for our ability to persevere, to grow, and to find joy in the unpredictability of life.

In embracing the art of letting go, we discover that control is but an illusion, a fragile construct that often stands in the way of true happiness and fulfilment. The journey toward releasing control is a journey home to ourselves, to a place of inner stillness and knowing where we understand that we are part of a larger tapestry, woven through with threads of destiny, choice, and chance. Here, in the heart of surrender, we find our true freedom—the freedom to live fully, to love deeply, and to embrace the vast, beautiful mystery of being alive.

But before we understand how to let go, we must understand why do we seek the control? At the heart of our quest for control lies a fundamental human instinct: the drive to mitigate uncertainty and protect ourselves from potential harm or discomfort. This urge, deeply embedded in our psyche, stems from our evolutionary roots, where survival depended on our ability to predict and influence our environment. In the modern context, though the stakes might differ, the underlying impulse remains the same—to navigate life's unpredictability with a sense of security and assurance. Understanding the reasons behind our need to control requires us to delve into the interplay between fear and desire—two powerful forces that shape our actions and motivations. Fear, whether of failure, rejection, or the unknown, often acts as the catalyst for our controlling behaviours. It whispers tales of doom should we step off the perceived safe path, compelling us to cling tighter to the illusion of control as a shield against the vagaries of fate. Conversely, desire—the longing for success, happiness, or fulfilment—fuels our attempts to orchestrate life's outcomes, convincing us that control is the key to achieving our dreams.

Beneath these surface motivations lies a deeper, more primal fear—the dread of powerlessness. To feel out of control is to confront our limitations, to face the humbling reality that, despite our efforts and intentions, external factors can sweep in and reshape our lives in an instant. This realisationcan evoke a profound existential unease, stirring questions about our place in the universe and the meaning of our endeavours. Yet, the compulsion to control not only springs from fear and desire but also from a misapprehension of what it means to live a fulfilled life. We are taught to equate happiness with achievement, peace with predictability, and success with the meticulous execution of our plans. This cultural narrative reinforces the notion that we are solely the architects of our fate, neglecting the role of chance, the influence of external forces, and the intrinsic value of the journey itself.

The urge to control, then, is a multifaceted phenomenon, rooted in our instinctual drive for survival, coloured by our deepest fears and desires, and shaped by societal constructs of success and fulfilment. Recognising these underlying factors is the first step in untangling ourselves from the grip of control, paving the way for a more open, trusting engagement with life's inherent uncertainty. As we continue to explore this theme, we will uncover how relinquishing control can lead not to chaos and vulnerability, but to strength, growth, and a deeper connection with the fluid dance of existence.

This intricate dance with control becomes more apparent when we examine the lives of individuals who embody both the struggle with and the release of control. Take, for example, a dedicated athlete, whose entire career is built on the premise of control—control over their body, their discipline, their technique, and ultimately, their performance.

The athlete's rigorous training schedule, strict diet, and mental preparation are all efforts to control as many variables as possible. Yet, despite their best efforts, factors outside their control—unexpected injury, adverse weather conditions during a competition, or simply an off day—can dramatically alter the outcome of their performance. The realisation that years of preparation can be upended by unforeseen circumstances can be a harsh lesson in the limits of control. Similarly, consider the corporate executive who meticulously plans their career trajectory, only to face industry disruptions or corporate restructuring that renders their plans obsolete. Or the diligent student who maps out their academic journey in detail, only to discover their passion lies in an entirely different field.

These scenarios unfold in countless lives, echoing the universal theme that while we can steer our ship with intention, we cannot calm the seas or command the winds. The athlete, the executive, and the student each face a choice in their moment of realisation: to cling tighter to the illusion of control, or to embrace the flow of life with openness and adaptability. Those who choose the latter often find a path rich with opportunities previously unseen, a testament to the paradox that in letting go of control, we often gain more than we relinquish.

Letting go of control does not mean abandoning goals or stop putting any effort. It is about acknowledging the fluid nature of life and our limited capacity to predict or govern every outcome. It involves shifting from a mindset of control to one of influence—recognising that while we can't control all aspects of our lives, we can influence many through our actions, attitudes, and responses. This shift allows for a more harmonious relationship with life's inherent uncertainties. Instead of bracing against the unknown with fear, we can approach it with curiosity and openness, allowing ourselves to be guided by experiences rather than trying to force them into preconceived moulds. It means finding peace in the present, even as we work toward future goals, and understanding that detours and unexpected outcomes are not failures but part of the rich tapestry of our lives. As we navigate the complexities of control, we learn that the true measure of our strength lies not in our ability to dictate every aspect of our journey but in our capacity to adapt, grow, and find meaning in the unpredictable flow of life. This realisation opens the door to a deeper form of freedom, one rooted in trust, resilience, and the courage to let life unfold in its mysterious, beautiful ways.

The Illusion of Control

The Illusion of Control deeply roots itself in the fabric of our existence, subtly dictating our choices, actions, and reactions to the unfolding tapestry of life. This pervasive belief—that through sheer will, meticulous planning, and relentless effort, we can steer the course of our lives in desired directions—shapes much of our experience. Yet, at its core, this belief is a mirage, a construct that, while comforting, obscures a more profound truth about our existence and our journey through it. At the heart of the illusion of control is the human tendency to overestimate our ability to influence events, outcomes, and even the actions of others. This tendency is not without its merits; it propels us forward, inspires innovation, and drives us to overcome obstacles. However, when left unchecked, it can become a barrier to spiritual growth, creating a false sense of security that distances us from the essence of life itself—its inherent uncertainty and impermanence.

The illusion of control hinders our spiritual growth in several key ways:

Resistance to Change: Life is in a constant state of flux, evolving and shifting in unexpected ways. The illusion of control fosters resistance to this natural ebb and flow, leading to rigidity and fear of change. Instead of embracing life's transitions as opportunities for growth and learning, we cling to outdated plans and expectations, missing out on the wisdom that comes from navigating the unknown.

Obstacle to Presence: By obsessing over controlling the future or ruminating on the past, we are pulled away from the richness of the present moment. Spiritual growth thrives in the "now"—in mindfulness, acceptance, and the full experience of being. The illusion of control keeps us anchored in a future that is not guaranteed, robbing us of the joy and lessons found in the present.

Barrier to Trust and Surrender: Fundamental to spiritual development is the ability to trust in a higher power, the universe, or the flow of life itself. This trust entails surrender—a letting go of the need to control every outcome and a faith in the journey's inherent goodness and purpose. The illusion of control makes this surrender challenging, as it is predicated on the belief that we alone are the architects of our fate.

Limits on Authentic Connection: Our relationships offer profound opportunities for spiritual growth, grounded in vulnerability, authenticity, and deep emotional exchange. The need to control can inhibit these connections, imposing expectations and restrictions that limit the free expression of self and others. True growth occurs in the space of acceptance and unconditional love—qualities that are often overshadowed by attempts to control the dynamics of our relationships. Recognising the illusion of control as just that—an illusion—marks a pivotal point in our spiritual journey. It invites us to release our grip on the reins of life, to open ourselves to the wisdom inherent in its unpredictability, and to embrace the liberating truth that while we may influence our path, we do not control it. This acknowledgment is not a resignation but a profound acceptance that liberates us to live more fully, love more deeply, and grow more authentically into the beings we are meant to be. This journey of understanding and releasing the illusion of control invites us into a deeper exploration of our own nature and the fabric of reality itself. It beckons us to question not only our desire for control but also the very essence of what it means to live a meaningful and fulfilling life. As we peel back the layers of this illusion, we uncover fundamental truths about our existence and our spiritual path.

The Paradox of Control: At the core of the illusion of control lies a paradox the more we strive to control life's variables, the more we encounter resistance and frustration. This struggle stems from a misalignment with the natural order, which is characterized by change, chaos, and complexity. Recognising this paradox invites a shift in perspective, from one of dominance to one of harmony. It teaches us that true empowerment lies not in controlling the external world but in mastering our internal responses to it. This mastery is the essence of spiritual resilience and growth.

The Gift of Uncertainty: While our instincts drive us to avoid uncertainty, it is within this space of not knowing that the greatest opportunities for growth and discovery lie. Uncertainty invites curiosity, flexibility, and innovation. It challenges us to remain open to the unexpected, to find comfort in the mystery, and to cultivate a sense of wonder about the journey of life. Embracing uncertainty as a gift rather than a threat enables us to experience life more fully, enriching our spiritual journey with insights and revelations that control would otherwise obscure.

Learning to Flow with Life: Releasing the illusion of control is akin to learning to flow with the currents of life rather than against them. This flow state is characterized by a deep trust in the process, an acceptance of what is, and a relinquishment of the need to predict and dictate every turn. It requires a profound faith in the inherent goodness of the universe and in our capacity to navigate its waters with grace and agility. Flowing with life opens us to experiences, connections, and paths we might never have considered, illuminating our spiritual journey with the light of the unforeseen and the serendipitous.

Deepening Our Connections: On a relational level, letting go of control fosters deeper, more authentic connections. It allows for the expression of vulnerability, the acceptance of imperfection, and the celebration of each individual's unique journey. These connections, grounded in mutual respect and understanding, become fertile ground for spiritual growth, offering reflections of our own nature and opportunities to learn about love, compassion, and the interconnectedness of all beings.

As we navigate the complex terrain of control and surrender, we are called to cultivate qualities of patience, humility, and courage. We learn to meet life with an open heart, to embrace each moment with gratitude, and to trust in the unfolding of our spiritual path. The process of releasing control is, ultimately, a journey back to ourselves—a rediscovery of our essence, untethered by fear and enriched by the boundless potential of a life lived in harmony with the universe.

In the delicate balance between holding on and letting go, my personal journey with control has been both enlightening and humbling. As someone who cherishes the act of planning, I have found a profound sense of comfort and security in mapping out the aspects of my life I believed were within my grasp. Take, for instance, the seemingly straightforward task of planning meals for the week—a task that epitomizes my love for organization and foresight. This ritual, methodical and satisfying, allows me to envision a week where nutrition and convenience harmonize, creating a seamless flow to daily life.

However, life, with its inherent unpredictability, has taught me the valuable lesson of discernment—the wisdom to recognise where my sphere of control ends, and the realm of acceptance begins. Despite my meticulous planning, there have been instances where not every item on my grocery list made it to my doorstep. Initially, such occurrences would stir a sense of frustration and a feeling of being upended by life's whims. It was a simple scenario, yet it encapsulated the broader theme of control and surrender that plays out across the various stages of our lives.

This seemingly mundane example became a microcosm for the larger, more complex situations where the line between what we can influence and what we must accept becomes blurred. It underscored the necessity of planning and effort—yes, we must take the steps that are within our power, laying the groundwork for the outcomes we desire. But it also highlighted the importance of flexibility and openness to the unexpected. The realisation that not every aspect of life will adhere to our plans, no matter how detailed or well-intentioned, became a gateway to deeper understanding and growth.

I have personally been attached to control a lot, letting go of control is a habit that is formed overtime. Navigating the early days of entrepreneurship, I was intimately acquainted with the tension between the need for control and the reality of life's unpredictable currents. One of the most palpable examples of this tension was the experience of waiting on a payment, with my bank account completely empty. Those days were a crucible, testing my resolve, my patience, and my ability to trust in the process. I found myself oscillating between hope and desperation, trying to will the situation into resolution, believing that through sheer determination, I could influence the outcome.

The lesson, however, did not lie in the exertion of control but in the act of release. Despite my efforts to secure the payment, to follow up, and to strategize, the resolution came in its own time, often after days or weeks of anxious waiting. The realisation dawned on me gradually: no amount of worrying or manipulation could accelerate the process. It was a profound lesson in the limitations of my control over life's broader strokes. The beauty, the relief, and the forward movement came only when I loosened my grip, when I acknowledged that the day would unfold as it was meant to, regardless of my attempts to steer its course.

This understanding was not an invitation to passivity or resignation but rather a call to a different kind of engagement with life—one that dances with the rhythms of existence rather than trying to lead at every turn. It was about recognising that delays, while frustrating, could also be detours pointing us in the right direction, that the unexpected could be a gateway to new opportunities and insights.

Incorporating what I had learnt about signs and the guidance of the Archangels into this journey transformed my approach. I began to seek their guidance, to look for signs, and to interpret the delays and challenges as messages rather than obstacles. This practice of seeking and heeding celestial guidance became a source of strength and comfort, a way to navigate the entrepreneurial journey with a sense of partnership with the divine.

Manifestation, belief, and surrender became the pillars of my approach. I learned to manifest with intention, to believe in the possibility of success and support, and most crucially, to let go of what was beyond my power. This did not mean abdicating responsibility or ceasing to act but rather acting with a sense of trust in the divine plan. It was an acknowledgment that while we play a crucial role in shaping our lives, we do so in concert with forces greater than ourselves, in a universe that moves with its own wisdom and timing.

Embracing this perspective has brought a sense of ease and grace to my journey. It has taught me that the true art of living lies not in mastering control but in mastering the art of surrender—to the flow of life, to the guidance of the angels, and to the belief in a divine plan that is always, in its essence, a dance of co-creation between the human and the celestial.

Over the years, I have learned to navigate this dance with control with a lighter step, embracing the duality of effort and surrender. While I continue to plan, to anticipate, and to prepare, I do so with the acknowledgment that the universe might have alternate arrangements. This acknowledgment doesn't diminish the value of planning; rather, it enriches it with a layer of wisdom and a touch of humility. It teaches us to hold our plans lightly, to be prepared to pivot when necessary, and to find peace in the understanding that some outcomes lie beyond our reach.

This journey towards embracing the balance between control and surrender has been transformative, guiding me to a place where planning meets trust, where effort aligns with acceptance. It has revealed that the essence of true control lies not in dictating every outcome but in mastering our reactions to the unfolding of life. In recognising the limits of our control, we open ourselves to the flow of existence, finding freedom in our ability to adapt, to accept, and to trust in the wisdom of a journey co-authored with the universe.

****

Once we begin to recognise the extent to which our desire for control permeates our lives, the next step on our journey is learning to let go of that control. This allows us to loosen the tight grip we often keep on the outcomes, about learning to trust in the flow of life with a deeper understanding that not everything can—or should—be controlled. The practice of letting go transforms our experience, ushering in a sense of freedom, peace, and alignment with the universe's rhythm.

Letting go of control can initially feel counterintuitive, perhaps even daunting. We might worry that by not holding on tightly, we are risking losing our way or that our desires will not come to fruition. However, the essence of this practice is not about loss but about gain—gaining an expansive sense of trust, a deeper connection to our intuition, and an openness to the possibilities life presents, even those we hadn't planned for.

Feeling the Release

As we practice letting go, the first thing many of us feel is a sense of relief. It is as if we have been holding our breath, bracing against the current of life, and suddenly, we allow ourselves to breathe freely. This relief is often accompanied by a newfound lightness, a release of the weight of expectations and the burden of needing to know and control every outcome.

Embracing Trust

Trust flourishes in the space vacated by control. It is a trust not just in the universe but in ourselves—in our resilience, our ability to navigate challenges, and our capacity for joy and creativity regardless of circumstances. This trust transforms fear into courage, allowing us to step into the unknown with a sense of adventure and openness.

Deepening Peace

Letting go cultivates a deep, abiding peace—a tranquillity that comes from understanding that we are part of a larger tapestry, woven together by threads of intention, chance, and interconnectedness. This peace doesn't insulate us from the challenges of life but equips us to meet them with grace, knowing that we are supported and guided, whether by our inner wisdom, the network of life around us, or the celestial guardians watching over us.

Experiencing Alignment

As we let go of the need to control, we find ourselves more aligned with the flow of life. This alignment feels like being in the right place at the right time, like the universe is conspiring to support us. It is the realisation that when we release our rigid expectations, we open ourselves to opportunities and blessings we couldn't have imagined.

Cultivating Openness

Finally, letting go nurtures an openness to the journey of life itself, to the beauty of its mysteries, and to the lessons embedded in every experience. We become students of life, eager to learn, grow, and evolve, no longer constrained by our need for certainty but enriched by our willingness to embrace the full spectrum of our existence.

In essence, the practice of letting go invites us into a more profound, harmonious way of being. It is a journey that requires patience, compassion, and courage, but one that promises to unfold the rich, vibrant fabric of life in ways we could never control or predict.

Meditation, a practice as ancient as it is profound, offers a gateway to inner peace, heightened awareness, and deeper connection to oneself and the universe. Rooted in the spiritual traditions of the East, meditation has traversed boundaries of culture, time, and belief systems to become a universal tool for cultivating mental, emotional, and spiritual well-being. The origins of meditation trace back thousands of years, with references found in the Vedas, ancient Hindu scriptures, indicating its practice as early as 1500 BCE. It has been a cornerstone of various Eastern philosophies and religions, including Buddhism, Taoism, and Jainism, each tradition offering its unique approach but all sharing the common goal of achieving a state of inner tranquillity and insight. At its core, meditation involves the deliberate focus of attention to quiet the mind's chatter, transcend the ego, and experience the present moment fully. This focus can take many forms, from the breath, a mantra, or a visual object to more contemplative practices that involve the cultivation of specific qualities such as loving-kindness or compassion.

Despite its ancient origins, meditation's relevance has only amplified in the modern world, where the pace of life and the constant bombardment of stimuli can lead to stress, anxiety, and disconnection from our inner selves. Meditation offers a respite from the noise, a space to breathe and reconnect with the stillness within.

The benefits of meditation are as varied as they are significant, ranging from reduced stress and improved emotional health to enhanced self-awareness, attention, and even physical health. Beyond these tangible benefits, meditation opens the door to spiritual exploration, inviting practitioners on a journey toward enlightenment, self-realisation, or a deeper understanding of the divine, depending on one's beliefs and aspirations.

In the context of letting go of control, meditation serves as a powerful practice for cultivating acceptance and surrender. Through the act of observing our thoughts and emotions without attachment or judgment, we learn to release our grip on the need to control, discovering instead a space of freedom and peace where life can unfold naturally.

More you explore meditation, it becomes clear that this practice is not merely an act of sitting in silence but a journey toward understanding the intricacies of the mind, the subtleties of existence, and the profound connection between the self and the universe. Meditation, in its myriad forms, invites us to explore the vast landscapes within us, offering pathways to tranquillity, insight, and transformation.

Techniques and Practices

Meditation encompasses a wide range of techniques, each with its unique focus and methodology, yet all converging on the common goal of fostering a deeper state of awareness and peace. Some of the most widely practiced methods include:

Mindfulness Meditation: Rooted in Buddhist tradition, mindfulness meditation emphasizes present-moment awareness, encouraging practitioners to observe thoughts, feelings, and sensations without judgment. This practice cultivates a state of open, attentive awareness, helping to break the cycle of habitual reactions and fostering a deeper appreciation for the richness of the present moment.

Concentration Meditation: This form involves focusing the mind on a single point of reference, such as the breath, a mantra, or a candle flame. The practice strengthens the mind's ability to concentrate, reducing the distractions that often lead to stress and anxiety, and paving the way for a deeper sense of inner calm.

Loving-Kindness Meditation (Metta): Aimed at cultivating unconditional love and compassion for oneself and others, Metta meditation involves silently repeating phrases of goodwill and kindness, gradually expanding this benevolent intention from close loved ones to all beings. This practice not only opens the heart but also fosters a sense of interconnectedness and empathy.

Body Scan Meditation: A component of mindfulness practice, the body scan involves paying detailed attention to different parts of the body, observing any sensations, tension, or discomfort without judgment. This technique promotes bodily awareness and relaxation, serving as a foundation for integrating mindfulness into everyday life.

Transcendental Meditation: A form of silent mantra meditation, Transcendental Meditation involves the repetition of a specific mantra given by a trained instructor. The practice aims to transcend thought and reach a state of pure consciousness, where the mind is free from activity, and a profound sense of peace and restfulness is achieved.

The Path to Letting Go

Meditation offers a powerful tool for recognising and letting go of the patterns of thought and behaviour that bind us. Through the practice of observing our inner experiences without attachment, we learn to disentangle from the narratives and fears that drive our need for control. This process of gentle observation and acceptance leads to a profound shift in perspective, where letting go becomes a natural expression of trust in the flow of life.

The beauty of meditation lies not only in its ability to reduce stress and enhance well-being but in its transformative potential. It invites us on a journey of self-discovery, where the layers of conditioning and illusion are peeled away, revealing the luminous essence of our being. As we cultivate a practice of meditation, we open ourselves to the wonders of existence, to the magic of the present moment, and to the freedom that comes from embracing life with an open heart and a trusting spirit.

Incorporating meditation into our daily lives becomes a sacred act of surrender, a dance with the divine, where each breath is a step closer to our true nature, each moment of stillness a window to the infinite. As we embark on this path, we find that letting go of control is not a loss but a liberation, an opening to the vastness of possibility and the depths of our own souls.

So, you must wonder, all this is great, but where do I start, and what if I couldn't remember to calm down? Embarking on the journey of meditation and learning to let go of control might seem daunting at first, especially if the concept feels foreign or if the mind refuses to quiet. The beauty of meditation, however, lies in its accessibility and simplicity. It is a practice that can be tailored to fit individual needs and lifestyles, starting with just a few minutes each day.

Beginning Steps:

- Begin with short meditation sessions, perhaps five minutes a day. The key is consistency rather than duration. Over time, as you become more comfortable with the practice, you can gradually increase the length of your sessions.

- Try to meditate at the same time each day. This could be first thing in the morning, during a lunch break, or before going to bed. A consistent routine helps establish meditation as a regular part of your day.

- Choose a quiet, comfortable spot where you won't be disturbed. It doesn't have to be a special room—just a corner of your living space where you can sit peacefully for a few minutes.

- Begin with a simple breathing meditation. Close your eyes, and take deep, slow breaths. Focus on the sensation of the air moving in and out of your body. When your mind wanders (and it will), gently bring your attention back to your breath.

- If you find it challenging to calm your mind on your own, guided meditations can be a helpful starting point. Numerous apps and online resources offer guided sessions that can lead you through the meditation process.

Addressing Forgetfulness and Restlessness

- Setting reminders on your phone or using a meditation app can help you remember to take time for your practice each day.
- It is normal for the mind to wander, especially when you are new to meditation. Rather than getting frustrated, acknowledge the distraction and gently redirect your focus back to your breath or the guided meditation.
- Meditation comes in many forms. If sitting quietly doesn't suit you, consider trying walking meditation, where you focus on the sensation of walking, or explore other mindfulness practices that might resonate more with you.

The initial steps into meditation and releasing control are less about perfection and more about exploration and curiosity. It is a personal journey, one that invites you to discover what works best for you. Remember, the goal of meditation is not to empty the mind of thoughts but to cultivate an awareness of the present moment, embracing it with acceptance and compassion.

As you integrate meditation into your life, you'll likely notice a shift—not just in your ability to calm your mind but in your overall approach to life's uncertainties. With practice, the moments of calm and clarity experienced during meditation begin to permeate other areas of your life, fostering a sense of peace and trust in the unfolding journey. This, in essence, is the beauty of beginning—a step into a world of greater mindfulness, connection, and freedom.

Embarking on the practice of meditation and the gentle art of letting go introduces us to a deeper layer of existence—self-awareness. This profound self-understanding is the bedrock upon which we build a more mindful, fulfilling life. Self-awareness allows us to observe our thoughts, emotions, and reactions without judgment, providing a clearer perspective on our intrinsic patterns and behaviours. Developing this awareness is essential, not just for personal growth but as a foundation for sustained meditation practice and the cultivation of a life less encumbered by the need for control.

Cultivating Self-Awareness

Mindful Observation: Begin by observing your thoughts and emotions as they arise, treating them as if you were a neutral bystander. This practice of observation without attachment helps to highlight the transient nature of your mental landscape, offering insights into your habitual patterns.

- Keeping a journal can be a powerful tool for developing self-awareness. Regularly write down your thoughts, feelings, and experiences. Over time, you'll begin to notice patterns, triggers, and perhaps even the root causes of certain behaviours or emotions.

- Ask yourself reflective questions about your actions and decisions. Why did I react this way? What does this emotion tell me about my needs or fears? This process of inquiry deepens your understanding of yourself and your motivations.

- Sometimes, our self-perception can be skewed. Open, honest feedback from trusted friends or family members can provide valuable perspectives on our behaviour and character traits we might not see.

- Empathy towards others can mirror back to our own experiences, feelings, and reactions, enhancing our self-awareness. By understanding others, we gain insights into ourselves.

Breath as a Gateway to Habitual Mindfulness

Amidst this journey towards self-awareness, the practice of focusing on the breath serves as a simple yet profound anchor to the present moment. Each inhalation and exhalation offer a reminder to return to the now, to ground ourselves in the reality of our direct experience. By taking a moment to breathe mindfully, especially when feelings of anxiety or the urge to control arise, we cultivate a space of clarity and calm within the chaos of daily life. To integrate this practice into a habitual part of your routine, start with intentional breaths at specific moments throughout the day—upon waking, before meals, or in moments of stress. These breaths serve as checkpoints, opportunities to pause and realign with the present.

As you continue to practice mindful breathing, you'll notice a shift. What begins as a conscious effort evolves into a natural part of your rhythm, a habitual return to mindfulness that weaves through the fabric of your day. This evolving practice not only deepens your meditation and enhances self-awareness but also becomes a stabilizing force, a source of inner peace amidst life's inevitable fluctuations.

Developing self-awareness and cultivating the habit of mindful breathing are intertwined paths leading towards the same destination—a life lived with greater presence, understanding, and acceptance. As you journey along these paths, remember that each step, each breath, is part of a broader tapestry of growth and discovery, revealing the beauty of letting go and the power of truly being in the moment.

Intuitive Creation

Moving beyond traditional practices and into the realm of unique techniques for releasing control, let's explore the transformative practice of "Intuitive Creation." This method combines elements of creativity, intuition, and mindfulness to foster a deeper connection with the present moment and to cultivate a space where letting go becomes a natural by product of the process. Intuitive Creation is about engaging with the creative process without a predefined plan or objective, allowing intuition to guide your actions. This practice can be applied to any form of creative expression—painting, writing, dancing, cooking, or even gardening. The focus is not on the outcome but on the act of creation itself, on being fully immersed in the moment, and on allowing your inner guidance to lead the way.

Steps to Practice Intuitive Creation

- Select a form of creative expression that resonates with you. It doesn't matter if you are skilled in it; what's important is your willingness to explore it freely.

- Create a space where you can engage in this practice undisturbed. You might play some gentle music, light a candle, or whatever else helps you feel relaxed and open.

- Before you begin, take a few deep breaths, and consciously release any expectations about the process or the outcome. Remind yourself that there's no right or wrong way to do this; It is all about exploration and expression.

- Start engaging with your chosen medium without a plan. Let your intuition guide your movements, your colours, your words, or your ingredients. If you find yourself thinking too much about what to do next, gently bring your focus back to the present moment and continue to let your intuition lead.

- As you create, observe the thoughts and feelings that arise without attaching judgment or analysis to them. Notice if the urge to control the process emerges and consciously choose to return to intuitive flow.

- After you have finished, spend a few moments reflecting on the experience. Consider what it felt like to let go of control and to allow your intuition to guide you. Reflect on any insights or emotions that arose during the process.

Intuitive Creation teaches us that letting go of control can lead to profound discoveries about ourselves and our potential for creativity and spontaneity. It reveals that within the space of surrender, there's a wellspring of inspiration, joy, and beauty waiting to be explored. This practice encourages us to trust in our inner wisdom, to embrace the unpredictability of the creative process, and to find peace in the knowledge that we are part of a larger, dynamic tapestry of existence.

By regularly engaging in Intuitive Creation, we cultivate a mindset that values presence, curiosity, and openness—qualities that enhance our ability to navigate life with grace and flexibility. This unique approach to letting go of control not only enriches our creative endeavours but also infuses our daily lives with a deeper sense of trust and flow, reminding us that sometimes, the most beautiful outcomes arise from the moments we least try to control.

Nature Immersion

Nature Immersion, my personal favourite, is a practice deeply rooted in human history, reflecting our intrinsic bond with the natural world. Historically, humans lived in close harmony with nature, intuitively understanding its rhythms and cycles. This ancient connection fostered a natural flow of living, guided by the seasons and the elements, teaching early humans the art of letting go and aligning with forces greater than themselves. In modern times, though many of us live removed from direct contact with the wild, the practice of reconnecting with nature remains a powerful pathway to release control and rediscover balance. I have found a profound sense of peace and grounding in connecting with water. Near my home, there is a small lake where I walk my dogs each morning. During these walks, I take time to observe the water, reminding myself to ebb and flow like its currents. Water, with its inherent fluidity and grace, serves as a perfect metaphor for the practice of letting go. It adapts to the contours of the land, flowing around obstacles with ease, yet possesses the strength to carve canyons over time.

This immersion in nature and the contemplative practice of observing water not only soothe the soul but also impart profound lessons on the essence of being. As I stand by the lake in the quiet of the morning, watching the gentle undulations of the water and feeling the cool earth beneath my feet, a deeper realisation unfolds within me: that life, in all its complexity and beauty, operates on principles of change and continuity, much like the water that flows without end. Each time I observe the water's surface, touched by the breeze or disturbed by a stone, I'm reminded of life's ripple effect—how our thoughts, actions, and states of being influence not just our immediate environment but extend outward, affecting the greater whole. This awareness brings a sense of responsibility and empowerment, highlighting the importance of our presence and how we choose to navigate the world.

Embracing the fluidity of water teaches us to approach life's challenges with a blend of strength and grace. Just as water can carve through stone not by force but by persistence, we too can overcome obstacles by staying true to our path, adapting as necessary, and maintaining a steady flow towards our goals. This lesson in persistence, coupled with the ability to let go and trust in life's timing, cultivates a resilience that is both gentle and unyielding.

The act of grounding ourselves, of physically connecting with the earth, reminds us of our place in the larger web of life. It is a humbling experience that invites a deep calm, born from the recognition of our interconnectedness with all beings and the planet itself. This sense of unity reinforces the understanding that our need to control often stems from a place of isolation and disconnection. Re-establishing our bond with nature serves as a powerful antidote, dissolving the barriers we have constructed and inviting us back into the communal dance of existence.

As we engage with nature, allowing its wisdom to permeate our being, we embark on a journey towards inner harmony. The lessons learned by the lakeside, in the forests, or under the expansive sky, become guiding stars in our quest to let go of control. They teach us that true strength lies in flexibility, that peace is found in acceptance, and that joy springs from the simple act of being fully present in the natural world.

This pathway of nature immersion, especially through the practice of observing and interacting with elements like water, offers more than just a technique for releasing control. It is a gateway to a profound transformation, a reawakening to the beauty of the present moment, and a reclamation of our inherent connectedness to the cosmos. By embracing the ebb and flow of life, like the ceaseless movements of water, we learn to navigate our journey with an open heart, a peaceful mind, and a spirit attuned to the infinite possibilities that unfold when we simply let go and trust in the flow.

How to Practice Nature Immersion

- **Mindful Walks:** Choose a natural setting for your walks, whether it is a park, forest, beach, or even your backyard. As you walk, pay attention to the sights, sounds, and smells around you. Notice the details of the leaves, the patterns of light and shadow, and the texture of the ground under your feet.

- **Grounding (Earthing):** Take a moment to stand barefoot on the earth, grass, or sand. Feel the connection between your feet and the ground, imagining roots growing from your soles deep into the earth, anchoring you in the present moment.

- **Water Connection:** If you have access to a body of water like a lake, river, or the ocean, spend time observing its movements. Notice how it flows freely, yielding yet powerful. Allow the qualities of water to inspire your practice of letting go, reminding yourself of the beauty and strength in flexibility and adaptability.

Connecting with nature in these ways can have a profound impact on our well-being. It reduces stress, enhances mood, and brings us into the present moment, reducing the incessant need to control our environment and outcomes. Nature teaches us valuable lessons in impermanence, resilience, and the interconnectedness of all life, guiding us towards a deeper understanding of ourselves and the world around us.

****

As we circle back to the essence of letting go of control, It is crucial to integrate this understanding into our daily lives, making it a conscious practice rather than a one-time realisation. The journey of relinquishing control and embracing the flow of life is ongoing, requiring gentle reminders and consistent effort. To foster this practice, drawing upon the wisdom of those who have navigated this path before us can be incredibly empowering.

One quote that resonates deeply in the context of letting go comes from the renowned spiritual teacher Eckhart Tolle, who insightfully observes:

> "Some changes look negative on the surface, but you will soon realise that space is being created in your life for something new to emerge."

This perspective invites us to view the act of letting go not as a loss but as a necessary clearing, a preparation for the new and beautiful to enter our lives.

Making Letting Go a Daily Habit

Below you will a sum up of the habits that you can integrate in your life to start your journey on letting go:

- **Morning Intention Setting:** Begin each day by setting an intention to remain open to the flow of life. Affirm to yourself, "Today, I choose to trust in the journey, staying present and open to the lessons it brings."

- **Mindful Reminders:** Throughout the day, use simple, mindful practices as reminders to let go of control. This could be as straightforward as taking a deep breath every time you check the time, using it as a cue to release tension and trust in the moment.

- **Gratitude Reflection:** End your day with a gratitude practice, reflecting on moments where you successfully let go and allowed life to unfold. Acknowledge these instances as steps towards deeper trust and surrender.

- **Journaling:** Keep a journal dedicated to your journey of letting go. Note your challenges, successes, and the insights you gain along the way. Writing about your experiences not only consolidates your learning but also serves as a reminder of how far you have come.

- **Nature Connection:** Regularly spend time in nature, as discussed earlier, allowing the natural world to reinforce the beauty and necessity of flowing with life rather than against it.

- **Community Support:** Share your journey with a supportive community or with friends who are also exploring the art of letting go. Discussing your experiences can provide mutual encouragement and insight.

By incorporating these practices into our daily lives, we cultivate an environment where letting go becomes more than just an idea—it becomes a lived experience, enriched by the peace and growth it brings. Remember, the process of releasing control is not about diminishing our power but about redirecting it towards living more harmoniously with the inherent uncertainty of life. It is about finding strength in vulnerability, wisdom in surrender, and profound freedom in the acceptance of life's ebb and flow.

In embracing this path, we open ourselves to a world where each moment is an opportunity for growth, where each challenge is a gateway to deeper understanding, and where letting go becomes the key to unlocking the fullness of our potential. As we continue to remind ourselves of the value of surrender, we find that life, in its infinite wisdom, guides us not towards what we thought we wanted, but towards where we truly need to be.

Chapter 5: Trusting the Journey

Trusting the journey—It is a phrase that rolls off the tongue with ease but assumes a weight of profound depth when we attempt to truly live by it. The concept of surrendering to the flow of life, of placing unwavering faith in the unseen workings of the universe, is both a challenge and an invitation. I am here, drawing from my own journey through the peaks and valleys of existence, to share with you a simple yet powerful truth: **everything unfolds precisely as It is meant to.** When your heart is aligned with joy and positivity, you become a magnet for goodness. However, It is in the stretches of life where the path blurs and shadows fall that our faith is truly tested. Embracing the unknown and trusting that our heartfelt desires will manifest in time requires a leap of faith—a belief in a benevolent universe that conspires in our favour, even when evidence to the contrary looms large. It is about understanding that our individual journeys are threads in a larger, divine tapestry, woven with the intent of leading us to where we need to be, not necessarily where we think we should be.

Why worry, indeed? Worry and doubt are but echoes of a mind that seeks to control, to forecast and script life's every outcome. Yet, the essence of trust lies in releasing these reins, in acknowledging that the wisdom of the universe far surpasses our own. When we ask for something, when we set an intention and release it into the cosmos, we must do so with an open heart, ready to receive in ways we might not anticipate. Trusting the journey does not mean inaction or passivity. Rather, It is an active engagement with life, where we do our part—planting seeds, nurturing our dreams—then step back and allow the universe to work its magic. It is a dance between making things happen and letting things happen, a balance that honours both our agency and the greater forces at play.

The beauty of trust is that it transforms fear into freedom, worry into peace. It teaches us that every moment of uncertainty, every detour, is part of a larger plan, meticulously crafted to lead us to our highest good. In times of doubt or when the wait seems endless, remember that the universe operates on its own schedule, one that is perfectly timed for the evolution of your soul.

So, as we journey forward, let us do so with trust as our compass, guiding us through the unseen, the unknown, and the unimaginable. Let this trust be a source of strength and serenity, a gentle reminder that even in the midst of chaos, a divine plan is unfolding, leading us not just toward what we desire, but toward where we are meant to be. Why worry, when we can believe, trust, and know that everything is, indeed, happening just as it should?

This trust in the journey, this faith in the universe's plan, becomes our beacon during the storms and our shade in the heat of life's trials. It is a declaration that, even in moments of uncertainty or when our paths seem to veer off course, there is a guiding hand, a cosmic orchestrator ensuring that every step, no matter how tentative, leads us closer to our true essence and destiny.

Cultivating Trust in Moments of Doubt

Inevitably, there will be times when our faith wavers, when the silence from the universe feels like abandonment rather than a lesson in patience. It is in these moments that trust becomes not just a spiritual concept but a practice—a conscious choice to believe despite the evidence, to hope despite the odds.

- **Reflect on Past Triumphs:** Remind yourself of the times when things fell into place, seemingly against all odds. These instances, whether big or small, serve as reminders that miracles do happen, and often, they occur right after we have surrendered our need for control.

- **Embrace the Lessons:** Every challenge or delay carries within it a lesson, an opportunity for growth. Trusting the journey means being open to these teachings, understanding that our spiritual evolution is often forged in the crucible of adversity.

- **Seek Comfort in Community:** Sharing your journey with others, especially those who embrace a similar faith in the universe, can provide comfort and reinforcement of your trust. These connections remind us that we are not alone in our struggles or our hopes. You can find Facebook groups or community circles in your area. If not, I encourage you to take the step to set up your own circles and invite others.

- **Nurture Your Spiritual Connection:** Whether through meditation, prayer, nature walks, or creative expression, strengthen your connection to the divine. This deepened bond becomes a source of strength and clarity, reminding you of the larger forces at play.

- **Let Go Daily:** Make a habit of consciously releasing your worries and desires to the universe each day. This act of letting go is a physical manifestation of your trust, a symbolic gesture of your faith in the divine plan.

The Divine Plan

As we navigate our lives, every joy, setback, encounter, and departure are a thread in the intricate tapestry of our existence, woven with divine precision. The beauty of this tapestry is only revealed when we step back, trusting in the artist's vision, understanding that each thread, no matter its colour or texture, contributes to the masterpiece of our lives. This journey of trust is not a one-time crossing but a bridge we build with every step, strengthened by our faith, our hopes, and our unwavering belief in the goodness of the universe. It is a path that leads us to discover not just the beauty of the world around us, but the luminous potential within us, waiting to be unleashed when we choose trust over fear, surrender over control.

In this dance with the divine, let us move with grace, with our hearts open to the music of the universe, confident that every step, every turn, is guided by love, leading us toward our highest selves. Trusting the journey is the ultimate act of faith, a profound acknowledgment that everything, indeed, is happening just as it should, in perfect harmony with the divine plan. Trusting the journey infuses our lives with a profound peace that is not easily shaken by external circumstances. This kind of peace whispers gently in the chaos, a steadfast reminder that beneath the surface turmoil, a deeper order and purpose are at play. It is a realisation that our essence, our very being, is not buffeted by the whims of fate but is part of a grand, divine orchestration moving us toward harmony, growth, and ultimate fulfilment.

Embracing this trust encourages us to live fully in the present, to immerse ourselves in the now with all its richness and complexity. We learn to let go of the heavy chains of past regrets and the anxieties that cloud our future, discovering instead the beauty and wisdom woven into the fabric of the immediate. It is in this state of presence that life truly unfolds, where joy is most palpable, and love finds its deepest expression. As we cultivate trust, we become more attuned to the subtle rhythms of life, learning to flow with its currents rather than against them. This doesn't mean passively resigning ourselves to whatever comes our way but rather engaging with life from a place of balance and wisdom. It is about doing our part, planting seeds for the future with hope and intention, while also being open to the unexpected twists and turns, knowing that sometimes, they lead us to destinations far richer than any we could have planned.

This approach to life, one of trust and openness, transforms our perspective on control. We begin to see control not as the ultimate goal but as a tool that, while useful, has its limits. It becomes clear that the tight grip we often seek to maintain on the reins of our lives can limit our capacity to experience the full breadth of what existence has to offer. Letting go of this need for control opens us up to new possibilities, to paths and potentials we might never have considered had we stayed rigidly attached to our predetermined plans. This is not a naive disregard for the realities of life. It is a deeply rooted belief in the underlying goodness and purpose of the universe, even when its ways are mysterious to us. It is a faith that, even in the darkest nights, stars of guidance and hope shine brightly, leading us through. This trust doesn't eliminate challenges or prevent missteps, but it does provide a compass by which to navigate them, a sense of assurance that, no matter how winding the path, it leads us home.

Thus, as we continue to traverse the landscapes of our lives, let us carry this trust as a lantern in the night, illuminating our steps with the gentle glow of faith. Let it remind us that, while we may not control the journey, we are never alone on the path, guided by a force far greater than ourselves, toward a destiny that unfolds in perfect timing, with wisdom and beauty beyond our comprehension. Trusting the journey means embracing life in its entirety, with all its uncertainties and surprises, as a dance with the divine, where every step, every turn, is part of a larger, magnificent ballet of existence.

All these concepts sound promising in theory, but what do they truly mean in the practical, everyday flow of our lives? Let me show you how this works in reality. The story is about someone I have known. Picture Sarah, a woman who recently faced a series of life-altering challenges. Six months ago, she lost her job unexpectedly, a role she had dedicated over a decade of her life to and found great fulfilment in. Not long after, she encountered health issues that not only drained her savings but also her spirit. Amidst these trials, her support system began to crumble, with friends and family seemingly distant when she needed them most. For Sarah, the world felt as if it were collapsing around her, each day heavier than the last, a relentless test of her resilience and faith.

In the depths of this turmoil, the concept of trusting the journey might seem not just difficult but almost inconceivable. How could one possibly find trust when every corner turned seems to lead further into the shadows?

For Sarah, the first step toward trusting the journey began with surrender—a letting go of the tight grip she had on her expectations of how life was supposed to unfold. This surrender wasn't immediate; it came in small moments, like the first deep breath after hours of anxious shallow breathing, or the first night of restful sleep after weeks plagued by insomnia. It was in these slivers of relief that Sarah began to find space—a space where her fears and worries weren't the sole occupants of her mind.

In this space, she found room for reflection. She started to see her situation not just as a series of unfortunate events but as a pivot point in her life's journey. She questioned, perhaps for the first time, whether her job had truly been fulfilling her deepest desires or if it had simply become comfortable. She considered her health scare as a stark reminder of her own mortality and the preciousness of each day. And the distancing of friends and family? It forced her to seek strength from within rather than relying solely on external support.

Sarah's journey to trust involved embracing uncertainty. She began to see the unknown not as a terrifying abyss but as a canvas of possibility. She took small steps, like pursuing a hobby she had always set aside for "someday" and reaching out to new communities that aligned with her evolving interests. Each step, though small, was a testament to her growing trust in the journey, an act of faith in a future she couldn't yet see but began to believe was there, waiting for her with open arms.

In this process, Sarah discovered the transformative power of gratitude. She started a daily practice of noting down things she was thankful for—even on her worst days. This practice didn't change her circumstances overnight, but it changed her. It shifted her focus from loss and lack to abundance and presence, illuminating the often-overlooked blessings that remained constant through her trials.

Months passed, and while Sarah's life hadn't miraculously righted itself, she found herself standing stronger, more resilient, and surprisingly hopeful. She realised that trusting the journey wasn't about passive waiting for things to improve but about actively engaging with life from a place of openness and faith. Her challenges hadn't disappeared, but her perspective had shifted dramatically. She no longer saw herself as a victim of circumstance but as a traveller on a journey, rich with potential for growth, learning, and rediscovery.

Trusting the journey, as Sarah learned, is about finding strength in vulnerability, wisdom in surrender, and an unwavering faith in the process. It is about understanding that sometimes, the path through the darkest valley leads to the most radiant dawn. For Sarah, and for anyone navigating their own storms, trusting the journey offers a beacon of hope—a reminder that even in the midst of turmoil, a divine plan is unfolding, guiding us not just toward what we want but toward where we need to be, transforming us into the fullest expression of ourselves.

Integrating the lessons of recognising signs, letting go of control, and trusting the journey forms a powerful trifecta for navigating life's complexities with grace and resilience. This holistic approach invites us to live more deeply, consciously, and in harmony with the universe's rhythms. It is about weaving these elements into the fabric of our daily existence, creating a tapestry rich with awareness, acceptance, and faith. Let's explore how these components come together to guide us in trusting the process of life.

Recognising Signs as Guideposts

Life continually presents us with signs—subtle nudges, coincidences, or even direct messages that, when observed and interpreted, can provide clarity and direction. These signs serve as guideposts, offering hints and reassurances from the universe that we are on the right path or suggesting adjustments when we stray. Integrating the practice of looking for and trusting in these signs encourages us to stay aligned with our true north, reinforcing our trust in life's journey. It teaches us to be present and attentive, to see beyond the surface chaos, and to find meaning in the patterns and synchronicities that unfold around us.

Letting Go of Control to Embrace Freedom

The act of letting go of control is fundamentally about embracing freedom—the freedom to live without the heavy burden of needing to dictate every outcome. This liberation opens us to the beauty of spontaneity, the richness of the unknown, and the peace that comes from faith in the natural course of events. It is about acknowledging our efforts and then releasing our attachment to specific results, trusting that whatever the outcome, it will contribute to our growth and well-being. This surrender is not a sign of weakness but a declaration of strength, a conscious choice to trust in the flow of life and to find balance between action and acceptance.

Trusting the Process as a Path to Peace

At the core of combining signs and surrender is the practice of trusting the process. This trust asks us to believe in the journey's inherent value, to see each experience as a step towards our evolution, and to have faith that the universe is guiding us towards our highest good. It is about seeing challenges as opportunities for learning, delays as divine timing, and unexpected turns as adventures leading us to where we need to be. Trusting the process imbues our lives with a sense of purpose and direction, even in moments of uncertainty, allowing us to navigate our days with a calm heart and a confident spirit.

Living the Integration

Living this integration means waking each day with the intention to remain open, to observe the signs with a curious and discerning eye, and to surrender the need for control with each breath. It is about cultivating a mindset that welcomes life's mysteries, that embraces each moment as an opportunity for discovery, and that holds space for the unexpected with trust and optimism.

It involves practical steps like pausing to reflect on the day's events, seeking the signs and lessons they might hold, and consciously releasing our worries and desires to the universe, reaffirming our trust in the process. It is a dynamic practice, one that evolves with us, deepening our connection to ourselves, to others, and to the divine orchestration of life.

As we journey forward, combining the wisdom of signs, the freedom of letting go, and the peace of trusting the process, we step into a way of living that is both empowering and humbling. We become co-creators with the universe, participants in a dance of divine timing and human effort, walking a path lit by faith and marked by a profound trust in the unfolding of our lives.
As we come to the end of this chapter, I would like to leave you with a practice that I personally use, It is called Synchronicity Mapping.

How to Begin Your Synchronicity Mapping Journey

- Choose a quiet and comfortable spot where you feel inspired and at peace. This space will be your sanctuary for reflection and creativity as you map out your journey.

- Have on hand a large piece of paper or a journal that resonates with you, along with coloured pens, markers, and any other artistic materials you are drawn to. These tools will help bring your map to life.

- Take some time to meditate or quietly reflect on the moments of synchronicity, the significant signs you have encountered, and the instances where letting go led to profound insights or shifts in your life.

Think about the times you have felt a deep, inherent trust in the flow of events, even when the path ahead seemed uncertain.

- Start plotting these moments on your map, allowing your intuition to guide the placement and the connections you draw between them. Use colours and symbols that hold personal meaning to express the emotions and insights tied to each event.

- As your map grows, take a step back to observe the patterns and pathways that emerge. Notice how instances of letting go intersect with moments of trust and how synchronicities seem to guide you along your journey. This visual representation serves as a powerful reminder of the interwoven tapestry of your life, highlighting the beauty and wisdom in surrendering to the journey.

- Synchronicity Mapping is an ongoing practice. Regularly update your map with new experiences and insights, watching as the tapestry of your journey unfolds in ever more complex and beautiful patterns.

- Use your map as a tool for reflection. Let it remind you of the journey you are on and the guidance you are receiving. Allow it to inspire trust in the moments when the path seems unclear, and to reinforce the value of letting go as a pathway to growth.

Synchronicity Mapping is a practice that invites you to engage with your life's journey in a deeply personal and visual way. It encourages mindfulness, gratitude, and a recognition of the interconnectedness of all things. As you embark on this practice, may it serve as a beautiful, living document of your growth, a testament to the trust you have placed in the journey, and a celebration of the mysterious, wondrous ways in which the universe guides and supports us all.

Navigating the spiritual journey, while deeply rewarding, can also surface various doubts and fears. These emotions are natural and almost inevitable as we explore the depths of our existence and confront the unknown. Understanding and addressing these common doubts and fears is crucial for growth and transformation on the spiritual path. Here's how we might approach them:

- Many of us question if we are on the "right" path or if such a path even exists. This doubt can stem from comparing our journey to others' or from societal expectations that don't align with our spiritual pursuits.

- Venturing into spiritual depths can lead us into uncharted territories within ourselves and the universe. The fear of what lies in the unseen can be a significant barrier to trust and surrender.

- Whether It is questioning the existence of a divine force, the efficacy of our practices, or the presence of guiding spirits or angels, doubts about the unseen support systems can shake our spiritual foundation.

- Spiritual growth often requires us to change, which might mean letting go of old identities, beliefs, or relationships. The fear of losing oneself or what's familiar can be daunting.

- Am I worthy of spiritual enlightenment? Can I truly manifest my intentions? Such doubts can undermine our trust in the journey and in ourselves.

Approach your spiritual journey with the heart of an explorer. Replace fear of the unknown with curiosity and openness to experience. This shift in perspective transforms the journey into an adventure where every experience, whether perceived as good or bad, offers growth and insight. Surround yourself with a community of like-minded individuals who share your spiritual aspirations. Sharing doubts and fears within a supportive group can help dispel them and reinforce your faith in the journey.

Practicing Self-Compassion

- Be kind to yourself when doubts and fears arise. Acknowledge them without judgment, understanding that they are part of the human experience. Self-compassion is a powerful tool for moving through emotional barriers.

- Remind yourself that spiritual growth is a process, one that unfolds in its own time. Cultivate patience and trust in this process, knowing that each step forward is a step toward greater understanding and enlightenment.

- When doubts and fears feel overwhelming, don't hesitate to seek guidance. Whether It is through meditation, prayer, consulting spiritual texts, or reaching out to a mentor, guidance is always available to those who seek it.

- Recall moments when you overcame challenges or when an unexpected turn led to a positive outcome. These reflections can bolster your trust in the journey and in the supportive forces guiding you.

Overcoming doubts and fears is not about eradicating them completely but about learning to navigate through them with grace and wisdom. It is about understanding that these emotions are signposts on the journey, guiding us toward deeper self-awareness and a more profound trust in the unfolding of our spiritual paths. By acknowledging, addressing, and integrating these lessons, we move closer to embodying the fullness of our spiritual potential, equipped with the strength, courage, and faith to embrace whatever comes our way on this beautiful journey.

Chapter 6: Transformation Through Surrender

As we reflect on our journey so far, learning to recognise signs, letting go of the need for control, and deeply trusting the path laid out before us, we arrive at a pivotal moment of realisation and potential: the transformative power inherent in the act of surrender. This is not merely another step in our spiritual journey; It is the essence, the core practice that unites everything we have explored into a coherent, meaningful whole.

Surrender is a profound release—a decision to open our hands and let the currents of life carry us where they will, not in passivity, but in full, vibrant participation with what is. This process, this decision to let go and trust, might sound simple, yet it marks the beginning of true transformation. But what does transformation through surrender truly look like? How does it unfold in the day-to-day reality of our lives? Transformation through surrender is an alchemical process. Like the alchemists of old who sought to transmute lead into gold, through surrender, we are invited to transform our challenges, fears, and perceived limitations into opportunities for growth, wisdom, and deeper joy. This transformation is not a passive occurrence; it demands our active participation, a conscious choice to meet each moment with openness and trust in the greater wisdom that guides our lives.

Part of this transformative process involves confronting and embracing our shadows—the parts of ourselves we might prefer to ignore or hide away. True surrender means accepting these aspects with compassion and understanding, acknowledging that they too are part of the intricate tapestry of who we are. In doing so, we don't resign ourselves to these shadows but rather integrate them, learning from them, and allowing them to inform our journey in positive, growth-oriented ways.

As we navigate this path, transformation manifests in various aspects of our being. Our relationships deepen and become more authentic as we learn to relate from a place of vulnerability and truth. Our decisions and actions align more closely with our core values and soul's purpose, as the noise of external expectations and societal pressures fades away. We discover a wellspring of creativity and inspiration within, unblocked by the fears and doubts that once held sway.

Moreover, surrendering to the journey reshapes our perception of challenges and obstacles. Rather than seeing them as barriers to our happiness or signs of failure, we recognise them as valuable lessons, catalysts for our evolution and stepping stones on the path to becoming more wholly ourselves. This shift in perspective is transformative in itself, altering how we experience life and interact with the world around us.

Trusting in the process, in the unseen guidance that leads us, becomes a source of strength and comfort. We learn to see the beauty in uncertainty, to find peace amidst change, and to cultivate a deep, unwavering faith in the journey's purpose and direction. This trust doesn't eliminate life's difficulties, but it does change how we move through them, imbuing our steps with grace, purpose, and a profound sense of alignment with something greater than ourselves.

The journey of transformation through surrender is ongoing, a perpetual unfolding of becoming and discovering. It is a path that calls us to live fully in each moment, to embrace life with all its complexities, and to find within ourselves the courage to let go and trust deeply in the flow of existence. As we continue to walk this path, let us do so with hearts open to the endless possibilities that surrender reveals, trusting that we are always exactly where we need to be, transforming, evolving, and emerging into the fullness of our being. This embrace of surrender doesn't just change us internally; it radiates outward, influencing our interactions, our choices, and the very essence of our daily lives. As we let go and trust more deeply, we find that our relationships begin to reflect this newfound openness and authenticity. Conversations become more meaningful, connections deeper, and our compassion for others and ourselves expands. We become beacons of calm in the storm, not because we are untouched by life's challenges, but because we have learned to navigate them with trust and grace.

Living in surrender also means our dreams and actions align more closely with our soul's true calling. Freed from the shackles of societal expectations and our own limiting beliefs, we dare to pursue paths that resonate with our deepest truths. Our work, our creativity, and our contributions to the world become reflections of our most authentic selves, infused with passion, purpose, and a profound sense of fulfilment. As we form a habit to trust and let go, we become more adaptable, resilient, and open to the flow of life. We learn to welcome change as a friend, understanding that it is the only constant in our journey. This flexibility allows us to embrace new opportunities, to grow through adversity, and to remain steady when everything around us is in flux.

One of the most beautiful aspects of transformation through surrender is the deep peace that comes with it—a peace that surpasses understanding. This peace is not the absence of trouble but a deep, inner calm that persists even in the face of uncertainty. It is a knowing that everything is unfolding perfectly, even if it doesn't align with our initial plans or desires. This peace is our anchor, keeping us grounded in the truth that we are exactly where we need to be, learning what we need to learn, and moving ever closer to who we are meant to become.

Embracing the journey of surrender and transformation invites us to live with our hearts wide open to the mystery and beauty of existence. It teaches us to see the sacred in the mundane, to find joy in the simple act of being, and to trust that every step, every breath, is part of a divine dance that moves us toward wholeness and harmony.

Moving forward let us carry with us the lessons of surrender, the courage to trust deeply, and the wisdom to let go. Let our lives be testament to the transformative power of embracing the journey, trusting in the unseen, and opening ourselves to the limitless potential that comes when we truly let go and allow the universe to guide us. This path of surrender is not always easy, but it is rich with rewards—leading us not only toward a deeper understanding of ourselves but also toward a greater connection with the world around us.

At a pivotal moment in my life, I found myself at a crossroads, staring into the heart of my own breaking point. It was a time when the pursuit of financial success had consumed me, weaving itself into the fabric of my being until I mistook its importance for the essence of my worth. Money, and the control I believed it exerted over my happiness and security, cast a long shadow over my spirit. But it was beneath this shadow that an awakening happened—a realisation that would alter the course of my journey and lead me to a transformation so deep, it was as if I had been reborn into a new existence. I came to understand that the control I had relinquished to material success was a chain of my own making. The constant chase, the endless cycle of want and material acquisition, left little room for the true essence of joy that had been waiting patiently within me, obscured by layers of societal expectations and personal fears. The decision to surrender to the divine plan, to release my grip on the illusion of control money held over my life, was not made lightly. But once made, it felt as though a weight had been lifted, allowing a light to shine through the cracks of my once armoured heart.

As my journey unfolded, a transformation began to take shape, not with the fanfare of sudden enlightenment, but as the gentle unfolding of a flower at the first hint of dawn. I discovered a wellspring of happiness that had always been inside me, independent of external circumstances or possessions. This happiness was not a fleeting sensation but a profound state of being, a deep contentment that flowed from an acceptance of life as it was, not as I had once insisted it should be.

The realisation that happiness is an inside job, that it blooms from the soil of surrender and trust, was liberating. I no longer sought validation or joy from outside events or the accumulation of wealth. Instead, I found glory in the simple, unadorned moments of life the warmth of the sun on my skin, the laughter of a loved one, the peace of a quiet morning. These experiences, once overlooked in my race for success, now took centre stage, each a testament to the beauty and richness of a life lived in harmony with the divine plan. This internal transformation was not just about finding happiness in new places; it was about rediscovering who I was beneath the layers of ambition, fear, and control. It was a journey back to my true self, a self that could find joy in being rather than having, in giving rather than acquiring. The path of surrender, of trusting in something greater than myself, had led me to a state of grace and gratitude I had never known before.

Sharing this personal transformation is not to say the journey was without its challenges or moments of doubt. Rather, It is to illuminate the profound shifts that can occur when we choose to let go, to trust in the unseen forces that guide our lives, and to find happiness within ourselves. It is a testament to the power of surrender, a reminder that when we release our need for control and open our hearts to the divine plan, we open ourselves to a world of beauty, joy, and deep, abiding contentment that no external achievement can provide. This transformation, born from the depths of surrender, is a journey back home to ourselves, a celebration of the light that shines within us all, waiting to be discovered.

The transformation that blooms through the act of surrender is not just a shift in perception but a profound change in how we experience life itself. It is akin to moving through the world with a new set of senses, ones attuned to the subtle whispers of the universe, the warmth of inner peace, and the luminosity of a soul in alignment with its true purpose. This journey of transformation through surrender is both deeply personal and universally resonant, echoing the timeless wisdom found in spiritual traditions around the globe.

Rumi, the 13th-century Persian poet and Sufi mystic, once said,

> "The moment you accept what troubles you have been given; the door will open."

This profound statement captures the essence of transformation through surrender. It is in the acceptance of our troubles, our challenges, and our fears that we find the key to a door we didn't even realise was closed. Beyond this door lies a realm of deeper understanding, connection, and joy—a place where the trials of life don't disappear but are met with a heart fortified by trust and eyes open to the beauty that emerges from struggle.

Feeling the Transformation

So, how do we feel this transformation? It begins in the quiet moments of surrender; in the spaces we create when we release our clenched fists and open our hands to the sky. It is felt in the deep sigh of relief when we realise, we no longer need to carry the weight of the world on our shoulders, that the universe is conspiring in our favour, even in ways we might not immediately understand. This transformation is also felt in our relationships, which begin to deepen and flourish in new ways. As we surrender our need for control and embrace trust, we allow others the space to be themselves fully, creating connections rooted in authenticity and love. We start to attract people and situations that resonate with our true selves, as if the universe is mirroring back the trust we have placed in it.

The transformation is evident in the choices we make. Decisions once rooted in fear or the desire for control give way to choices made from a place of love, intuition, and trust. We begin to live more courageously, aligned with our values and dreams, because we know that even in uncertainty, there's a guiding force leading us toward our highest good.

Practical Steps to Cultivate Transformation Through Surrender

- Take time each day to reflect on where you might be holding onto control and gently remind yourself to trust and let go. Journaling can be a powerful tool in this practice.

- Engage in mindfulness practices and meditation to cultivate presence and deepen your connection to the present moment, where true surrender and trust flourish.

- Draw inspiration from spiritual texts, nature, art, or the wisdom of those who have walked this path before you. Let their journeys remind you of the transformative power of surrender.

- Surround yourself with a community that supports your journey of transformation. Sharing experiences and insights can reinforce your trust in the process.

As we continue to navigate our paths, let us remember that transformation through surrender is not a destination but a way of being, a continuous unfolding of our most authentic selves. It is a dance with the divine, a song of the soul, inviting us to let go, trust deeply, and open ourselves to the miraculous unfoldment of our lives. In this surrender, we find not just peace and joy but a profound sense of coming home to ourselves, to a life lived in harmony with the universe's perfect, mysterious plan.

This journey of transformation is an ever-evolving process, marked not by a series of destinations but by the richness of each step, each breath, and each moment of surrender. As we venture deeper into this path, we discover that surrendering to the divine plan is not about losing ourselves but about finding ourselves in the most authentic way possible. It is a process of peeling back the layers of who we thought we needed to be to uncover the truth of our being, radiant and whole, beneath.

In this space of surrender, our perception of the world around us shifts. We start to see the magic in the mundane, the extraordinary in the ordinary. A walk in the park becomes a dialogue with the divine; a conversation with a stranger reveals messages from the universe; our very dreams become clearer, infused with the guidance and wisdom we have opened ourselves up to by trusting the journey.

The transformation through surrender also deepens our resilience. We become like trees, deeply rooted in our essence yet flexible enough to sway with the winds of change. This resilience is born from an inner strength that knows the difference between what we can change and what we must accept. It gives us the courage to face life's storms, not because we are impervious to pain, but because we trust in our ability to navigate through it, to grow from it, and to emerge on the other side with new rings of wisdom in our core.

Moreover, as we embody this transformation, our very presence becomes a beacon for others. Our journey of surrender, with all its trials and triumphs, becomes a testament to the power of faith and the beauty of a life lived in harmony with the universe's rhythms. We inspire those around us not by preaching about trust and surrender but by living it, by embodying the peace and joy that come from this deep alignment with life's flow.

The art of transformation through surrender asks of us one simple, yet profound, commitment: to remain open to the unfolding of our lives, to greet each day with a heart willing to receive whatever lessons, blessings, and challenges it may bring. It invites us to trust deeply in the unseen forces that guide our journey, to believe in the wisdom of our soul's path, and to find peace in the knowledge that everything is unfolding exactly as it should.

This profound surrender, this gentle release of our insistence on control, naturally steers us towards a state of being where trust is not just a concept, but a lived experience. In this state, we find ourselves more receptive to the lessons life offers us, more appreciative of the present moment, and more connected to our own essence and to the world around us. Surrender does not mean giving up our dreams or desires; rather, it means pursuing them with an open heart, ready to receive guidance and to accept outcomes, even when they diverge from our meticulously laid plans.

In the heart of surrender, there's a quiet but potent realisation that our true power lies not in our ability to control everything but in our capacity to flow with life's inherent uncertainty. This realisation frees us from the shackles of worry and fear, allowing us to live more fully, to love more openly, and to embrace each day with renewed wonder and gratitude. It teaches us that resilience is not about standing rigid against the storm but about bending gracefully with the wind, secure in the knowledge that our roots are deep and our ability to adapt and grow is infinite.

As we deepen our practice of surrender, we begin to notice subtle shifts in our everyday life. Challenges that once seemed insurmountable now appear as opportunities for growth; what once triggered anxiety now invites a pause for reflection and a recentring of our trust. We start to understand that every obstacle is a stepping stone, every setback a redirection towards paths we might never have explored otherwise. Our journey serves as a reminder of the transformative power of trust and acceptance. In sharing our story, in living our truth, we offer a light to those still navigating their way through the darkness, showing that there is a path forward, illuminated by faith and graced with the promise of renewal and growth.

Let us then carry this practice of surrender into each day, weaving it into the fabric of our lives with intention and love. Let it be our guide through times of change and our anchor in moments of stillness. And as we move forward, may we remember that the act of surrendering to the journey, with all its twists and turns, is itself a profound act of courage, a testament to the strength of the human spirit, and a celebration of the boundless potential that lies within each of us when we choose to trust, to let go, and to allow the divine tapestry of our lives to unfold in its perfect, mysterious timing.

The process of transformation

The process of transformation through surrender can be envisioned as a journey through various stages, each bringing its own challenges and revelations. This transformative journey not only deepens our spiritual connection but also facilitates profound personal growth. By understanding these stages, we can navigate the path of surrender with greater awareness and intention.

Stage 1: Recognition and Acknowledgment

This initial stage is foundational and perhaps the most crucial. It involves a deep inward journey, a process of becoming acutely aware of the facets of our lives where the grip of control is tightest. This recognition often comes during moments of quiet reflection or amidst life's challenges when the patterns that no longer serve us become glaringly evident. It is a period of awakening, where we begin to see the distinction between healthy ambition and the compulsive need to control outcomes. Acknowledgment requires humility and courage, as it often means confronting uncomfortable truths about ourselves and our limitations.

Stage 2: Willingness to Change

Once we recognise and acknowledge the areas of our lives stifled by our need for control, we arrive at a crossroads. The willingness to change is a pivotal moment of choice—It is where we decide to open ourselves to new possibilities and ways of being. This stage is characterized by an internal shift, a softening of the heart, and an openness to explore paths less travelled. It is about saying "yes" to the journey ahead, even without knowing where it will lead, fuelled by the understanding that there has to be a more harmonious way to navigate life.

Stage 3: Active Surrender

Active surrender is where intention transforms into action. It is one thing to desire change and another to embody it. This stage involves practical steps: perhaps starting a meditation practice, seeking guidance through therapy or spiritual direction, or simply incorporating moments of stillness into our daily routine. Active surrender is a commitment to trust in the face of uncertainty, to accept without resignation, and to engage with life from a place of openness and receptivity. It is marked by daily choices that align with letting go and trusting the process, reinforced by rituals that remind us to release our hold on the reins.

Stage 4: Experiencing Release

The fruits of active surrender become apparent in this stage. Experiencing release is often described as feeling a weight lifted off one's shoulders. It is a stage where the struggle with control begins to ease, and we start to witness the benefits of our surrender. Stress and anxiety diminish as we learn to navigate life with trust and acceptance. There's a newfound freedom in this release, a joy in discovering that life can unfold beautifully without our constant interference. This stage reaffirms our faith in surrender, showing us that letting go is not about losing but about gaining a deeper sense of peace and alignment with our true selves.

Stage 5: Deepening Trust and Connection

As we experience the release that comes from surrender, our trust in the journey deepens. This stage is characterized by a profound connection to the flow of life, to ourselves, and to something greater than us—be it the universe, nature, or the divine. Trust becomes our foundation, influencing how we make decisions, face challenges, and relate to others. It is a trust that doesn't negate the realities of pain or difficulty but offers a way to navigate them with grace and resilience. Our connections become more authentic, rooted in vulnerability and shared humanity, enriching our lives and those around us.

Stage 6: Transformation and Integration

The culmination of our journey, transformation and integration, is where the changes wrought by surrender are fully realised and become integral to our being. This transformation touches every aspect of our lives, altering how we see the world, engage with others, and understand ourselves. We integrate the lessons learned through surrender, embodying a way of being that is fluid, responsive, and deeply grounded in trust. This stage is not an end point but a platform for ongoing growth, a state of openness to continual evolution, and an invitation to live in constant alignment with the dynamic tapestry of life.

Each stage of this journey offers unique insights and challenges, guiding us toward a fuller, more authentic expression of ourselves. As we navigate these stages, we learn that transformation through surrender is not just about personal growth but about how we contribute to the world from a place of deepened understanding, compassion, and love. It is natural for questions to arise during the process, each seeking to bridge the gap between understanding and practice. These questions are not just queries; they are beacons that light our path, guiding us deeper into the essence of what it means to truly let go and trust the journey. Whether you are standing at the threshold of surrender, or you find yourself wrestling with the nuances of letting go amidst life's inevitable challenges, the questions that surface are a vital part of the process. They invite us to explore, to reflect, and ultimately, to deepen our commitment to this path of surrender. In addressing these inquiries, we embark on a dialogue with our deepest selves, uncovering insights and affirmations that bolster our faith in the transformative power of surrender.

1. How do I know if I'm truly surrendering or just being passive?

True surrender is an active choice to trust and let go of the need to control outcomes, distinguished from passivity by its foundation in trust and intention. When you surrender, you are engaging with life consciously, making decisions and taking actions aligned with your values, while being open to the outcomes, knowing you have done your part and the rest is up to the universe. Passivity, on the other hand, involves disengagement and a lack of initiative, often stemming from fear or indifference.

2. Can surrendering make me lose my drive or ambition?

On the contrary, surrendering can refine and redirect your drive and ambition towards pursuits that are more in harmony with your true self. It removes the noise and pressure of external expectations, allowing your genuine passions and interests to guide you. This leads to a more fulfilled and purpose-driven life, where your ambitions are fuelled by joy and inspiration rather than fear or competition.

3. *What if I surrender and things don't improve?*

Surrendering is not a magic solution that instantly resolves all challenges, but a practice that changes how you perceive and navigate life's ups and downs. The improvement lies in your increased resilience, peace, and the ability to find joy and lessons in all circumstances. Trusting the journey means understanding that every experience, whether perceived as good or bad, contributes to your growth and leads you to where you need to be.

4. *How can I practice surrender when I'm anxious or afraid?*

Surrendering amidst anxiety or fear requires gentle steps. Start with mindfulness practices to ground yourself in the present, such as focused breathing or meditation. Acknowledge your fears without judgment, then consciously choose to release them, even if just for a moment. Remind yourself of times when letting go led to positive outcomes, reinforcing your trust in the process. Over time, these practices can help ease anxiety and cultivate a habit of surrender.

5. *Is it possible to completely let go of control?*

Letting go of control is a journey with varying degrees of surrender. Complete relinquishment of control is not necessarily the goal, nor is it entirely feasible, as we have responsibilities and choices to make. The aim is to find a balance, where we do our part yet remain open to the outcomes, understanding that some aspects of life are beyond our control. It is about striving for a state where our need to control doesn't consume us, allowing for greater peace and trust in life's flow.

The path of surrender is both personal and universal, etched into the fabric of our individual experiences yet reflective of a collective longing for peace, connection, and alignment with a greater flow. It beckons us to shed the layers of fear, expectation, and control that constrain us, urging us to step into the vastness of our true potential. As we journey through this process, we discover that surrender is not about losing ourselves but about coming home to ourselves, embracing the essence of who we are beyond the confines of ego and attachment.

This journey transforms us, not by altering the external landscapes of our lives, but by shifting our internal perspective, offering us a lens of trust and acceptance through which to view the world. We learn to see challenges as teachers, obstacles as opportunities, and endings as beginnings. We find beauty in the impermanence of life, recognising that each moment, each breath, is a gift—an invitation to engage with the richness of existence.

As we move forward, let us carry the lessons of surrender with us, not as burdens but as beacons. Let them illuminate our path, guiding us through darkness and doubt, reminding us of the strength, wisdom, and grace that lie within our willingness to let go. Let us embrace the unknown with open hearts, knowing that the journey ahead, though uncertain, is replete with possibilities for growth, joy, and fulfilment. In surrendering, we align ourselves with the rhythms of the universe, becoming co-creators in the masterpiece of our lives. We learn to flow with the currents of existence, finding in this flow a profound sense of harmony and purpose. This alignment brings us closer to our authentic selves, to each other, and to the divine, weaving a tapestry of connection and meaning that transcends the boundaries of our individual experiences.

Chapter 7 Living In Grace

As we turn the pages of our journey together, we arrive at a chapter that seeks to illuminate the path to living in grace—a concept as timeless as it is transformative. Up until this point, we have navigated the realms of recognising signs, embracing the art of letting go, and the profound act of trusting the journey, each step revealing deeper layers of our spiritual and personal evolution. Now, we venture into the heart of what it means to incorporate grace into our daily lives, weaving the essence of grace into the very fabric of our existence.

Living in grace is an invitation to move through the world with an open heart, to face each day with compassion, and to engage with life's challenges and blessings with a spirit of gratitude and humility. It is about recognising that grace is not just a fleeting moment of divine intervention but a constant presence that guides, supports, and illuminates our path. This chapter aims to bridge the lessons we have learned so far, showing how the surrender to divine timing, the acknowledgment of signs, and the trust we place in the journey are all expressions of living in grace.

To live in grace is to understand that every moment of our lives is infused with meaning, even those that seem mundane or challenging. It is to see the beauty in the imperfection, the lessons in the trials, and the opportunities for growth in every encounter. Grace teaches us to view life not as a series of random events but as a carefully orchestrated dance, where each step, each turn, is an opportunity to embody love, kindness, and understanding.

Incorporating grace into our daily lives means making decisions that reflect our highest values, acting with integrity even when no one is watching, and extending kindness not just to others but to ourselves. It involves maintaining a connection to the divine, however we conceive it, allowing this connection to guide our thoughts, actions, and interactions with the world. Living in grace is about moving through life with a sense of ease and assurance, knowing that we are supported by something greater than ourselves, that every challenge is an opportunity for deepening our faith, and that every joy is a reminder of life's boundless gifts.

As we explore what it means to live in grace, we'll delve into practices that can help us cultivate this way of being, from mindfulness and gratitude to acts of service and the conscious cultivation of positive relationships. We'll discover how living in grace doesn't require us to change who we are but to become more fully who we are meant to be, aligning our inner world with the outer in a harmonious balance.

Through personal reflections, stories of transformation, and practical guidance, this chapter invites you to step into a state of grace, to experience life with a renewed sense of wonder and a deepened connection to the divine. Let us embark on this journey together, with open hearts and minds, ready to embrace the grace that awaits in every moment, guiding us towards a life of fulfilment, purpose, and profound joy.

One of the most profound daily practices for incorporating grace into your life is the practice of Gratitude Reflection. This seemingly simple act has the power to transform your perspective, nurture your soul, and open your heart to the abundance of grace that surrounds you. Gratitude is the gateway to grace; it shifts our focus from what we lack to the infinite blessings that enrich our lives, fostering a sense of contentment and a deeper connection to the divine essence of existence.

Gratitude Reflection: A Daily Practice

- Start your morning by reflecting on three things you are grateful for. These can be as simple as the warmth of your bed, the sound of birds singing outside your window, or the presence of a loved one in your life. The act of recognising these blessings upon waking sets a tone of appreciation and openness for the day ahead.

- Choose a small object, such as a stone, coin, or piece of jewellery, as your gratitude token. Carry it with you throughout the day as a tangible reminder to pause and acknowledge moments of grace and beauty. Each time you touch or see this token, take a brief moment to mentally note something you are grateful for at that moment.

- End your day by jotting down in a journal the moments of grace you encountered, no matter how small or seemingly insignificant. Reflecting on your day through the lens of gratitude can shift your perspective, highlighting the abundance of blessings that enrich your life. It is a practice that not only nurtures a grateful heart but also cultivates a deeper connection to the present moment and the beauty it holds.

For those interested in a structured approach to cultivating this daily practice of gratitude, I have created "My Magnificent Day" journal, available on Amazon in both kids and adult versions. This journal offers guided prompts and spaces designed to help you recognise, reflect on, and celebrate the grace-filled moments of your day, fostering a deeper appreciation for life's gifts. Whether you are just beginning your journey into gratitude or looking to enrich your existing practice, "My Magnificent Day" journal can be a valuable companion, guiding you towards living each day with a fuller, more grateful heart.

Living in grace fundamentally transforms how we approach decision-making in our lives. It is about aligning our choices with the deepest truths of our being, ensuring that each decision reflects not only our values and integrity but also our commitment to moving through the world with a spirit of compassion and understanding. This practice of **Graceful Decision-Making** is a conscious approach to navigating life's crossroads with wisdom and heart.

Graceful Decision-Making: A Daily Practice

- Before making a decision, take a moment to centre yourself. This can be a brief period of meditation, deep breathing, or simply sitting in silence. The goal is to connect with your inner sense of calm and clarity, creating a space where your decisions can emerge from a place of inner alignment rather than external pressure or fleeting emotions.

- Engage in reflective questioning. Ask yourself, "Does this choice reflect my true values? Will it bring me closer to the person I aspire to be? How does this decision impact those around me?" By contemplating these questions, you encourage choices that resonate with the

227

essence of living in grace—those that nurture growth, foster kindness, and contribute to a greater good.

- Every decision we make sends ripples through our lives and the lives of others. Part of making choices in a state of grace involves considering the wider consequences of our actions. Imagine the potential outcomes your decision might create, not just for you, but for the community and environment around you. This broader perspective can guide you towards decisions that are harmonious and beneficial on multiple levels.

- Graceful decision-making recognises that we cannot always predict the outcomes of our choices, but we can trust in the process. Embrace uncertainty by reminding yourself that each decision is a step on your journey, an opportunity to learn and grow. Trust that, by making choices aligned with your highest self, you are being guided along a path that is meant for you, even if it takes unexpected turns.

- After making a decision, take time to reflect on its impact and how it felt to make it. Was there a sense of peace or discord? Reflection is a crucial part of graceful decision-making, as it allows us to learn from our experiences and adjust our approach in the future. It is about being gentle with ourselves, acknowledging that making mistakes is part of the journey, and each misstep is a chance to realign with grace.

By incorporating these practices into our daily lives, we learn to make decisions that are not only good for us but also serve the greater good, reflecting our commitment to living in grace. This approach to decision making enriches our lives, deepening our connections with others and with the world around us, and guiding us towards a life that is more meaningful, balanced, and joyfully lived.

Affirmation Practice for Trusting Divine Timing

Integrating affirmations into our daily routine can be a powerful practice to reinforce the principles of living in grace, especially when we remind ourselves that "Everything is as it should be" or that "Everything is working out in divine timing." These affirmations help us cultivate trust and patience, reminding us of the larger, harmonious flow of the universe that we are part of. Let's explore a practice cantered around these affirmations to deepen our sense of grace and trust in life's unfolding.

- Begin each day by setting a positive tone with your chosen affirmation. Upon waking, before you even get out of bed, close your eyes and take a few deep, grounding breaths. Silently or aloud, repeat to yourself, "Everything is as it should be, unfolding in perfect divine timing." Visualise these words enveloping you in a warm, comforting light, instilling a deep sense of trust and peace within you.

- To keep this affirmation, present in your mind throughout the day, create visual reminders for yourself. This could be a sticky note on your bathroom mirror, a wallpaper on your phone, or a small card tucked into your wallet. Each time you encounter this reminder, pause for a moment to repeat the affirmation in your mind, reinforcing the practice of trust and acceptance.

- Set aside a few moments in the middle of your day—perhaps during a lunch break or a quiet moment—to reconnect with your affirmation. Find a quiet space to sit comfortably and reflect on the first half of your day. Acknowledge any moments where you felt out of alignment with the idea that everything is unfolding as it should. Gently remind yourself of your morning affirmation, allowing it to re-centre and guide you through the rest of the day with grace and trust.

- End your day with a reflective practice focused on your affirmation. Before going to sleep, recall instances throughout your day where you felt the truth of your affirmation, moments when you could see the divine timing at work in your life. Acknowledge and give thanks for these instances, however small they may be. This practice not only deepens your trust in the flow of life but also cultivates a sense of gratitude for the journey, with all its twists and turns.

- For those inclined to journaling, dedicating a section of your journal to explore and document how this affirmation manifests in your life can offer deeper insights. Write about the moments when trusting in divine timing was challenging and the moments when it brought you peace or unexpected blessings. Reflecting on these experiences can reinforce your faith in the affirmation and provide personal evidence of its truth in your life.

Incorporating this affirmation practice into your daily routine is a gentle yet powerful way to remind yourself of the beauty of surrendering to the flow of life, trusting that everything is indeed as it should be, unfolding in perfect divine timing. Through this practice, we learn to navigate life with a deeper sense of calm, trust, and grace, opening ourselves to the wisdom and blessings that each moment brings.

Living in grace, especially under pressure or during challenging times, requires a conscious effort to return to a state of trust and acceptance. It is easy to forget the principles of grace when faced with deadlines, conflicts, or any stressors that push us towards reactive patterns. Recognising these moments as opportunities to practice grace under pressure can transform our experience and lead us to a deeper understanding and resilience. Here are some practical examples and strategies for maintaining grace in the midst of life's inevitable pressures:

Example 1: Facing a Tight Deadline at Work

Under the pressure of a looming deadline, stress levels can skyrocket, leading us to operate in a mode of panic and control. In these moments, pause and take a deep breath. Remind yourself, "I am doing the best I can with what I have." Allow this affirmation to centre you, then approach your work with focused attention, doing one task at a time. This mindful approach can help mitigate overwhelm, enabling you to work efficiently while maintaining an inner sense of calm and grace.

Strategy: Schedule short breaks to breathe and recentre yourself. Use these moments to reflect on your progress, not just on the tasks remaining. This practice can help shift your perspective from one of scarcity to one of abundance and capability.

Example 2: Navigating Conflict in a Relationship

Conflict, especially with loved ones, can quickly lead us away from grace, drawing us into reactions driven by hurt or anger. In these instances, living in grace means taking a step back to listen actively and empathetically, even when every instinct might be urging you to defend or counterattack. Remember that grace in relationships involves seeking understanding and common ground, not just proving a point.

Strategy: Before responding in a heated moment, take a few deep breaths and remind yourself of the love or respect that underpins your relationship. Ask yourself, "How can I address this situation with kindness and clarity?" This pause can make a significant difference in the outcome of the conflict.

Example 3: Dealing with Personal Setbacks

Personal setbacks, whether in goals, health, or any other area, can shake our faith in the journey. It is during these times that grace can seem most elusive. Yet, it is precisely here that grace becomes most vital. Reminding yourself that setbacks are not failures but part of the path can help you navigate these moments with dignity and resilience.

Strategy: Reflect on past setbacks that eventually led to growth or unexpected opportunities. Use these memories as a foundation to build your trust in the present situation, understanding that grace often manifests in the guise of challenges.

Maintaining grace under pressure is an art form, a delicate balancing act that requires mindfulness and a profound connection to our inner reservoir of peace and acceptance. This is not about adhering to a strict set of practices or rituals but rather about cultivating an inner landscape where grace naturally flourishes, even amidst the tumult of life's demands and challenges.

Imagine grace as a tranquil river flowing through the heart of a bustling city. Around it, the pace of life is frenetic, filled with the clamour of deadlines, conflicts, and expectations. Yet, the river remains serene, its waters moving with a gentle, unwavering grace. This river is within us, a metaphor for our capacity to maintain composure and kindness in the face of life's pressures. It is about finding that quiet centre within ourselves, where we can return for renewal and perspective whenever the outside world becomes overwhelming.

To live in grace under pressure, then, is to cultivate an awareness of this inner sanctuary and to learn how to access it readily. It is about recognising the signs of mounting stress or disconnection and gently guiding ourselves back to a state of equilibrium. This might mean pausing in the middle of a hectic day to take a few deep breaths, reminding ourselves of our deeper values and commitments, or simply choosing to respond to a challenging situation with empathy rather than irritation.

The beauty of living in grace is found in these moments of choice. When under pressure, the choice to respond with patience, to listen actively, or to offer a word of encouragement can be transformative, not just for us but for those around us. These choices ripple out, affecting our environments and relationships in profound ways. They remind us that grace is not a static state but a dynamic way of engaging with the world, one that enriches our lives with meaning, connection, and peace.

Furthermore, sharing our experiences of grace under pressure can be a powerful way to inspire and uplift others. It is in the sharing of our stories that we reveal the possibility of a different way of being, one that embraces the complexities of life with an open heart and a spirit of trust. By modelling grace in action, we contribute to a collective energy of resilience, compassion, and understanding, reinforcing the idea that grace is not just an individual practice but a shared human experience.

Living in grace is a journey that unfolds moment by moment, choice by choice. It is a commitment to approaching life with an open heart, a clear mind, and a spirit attuned to the beauty and lessons that each experience brings. In doing so, we not only navigate life's pressures with greater ease and joy but also inspire those around us to discover the grace within their own lives. This path of grace is not always easy, but it is rich with rewards—leading us not only toward a deeper understanding of ourselves but also toward a greater connection with the world around us.

Chapter 8 – Moving Forward in Faith

As we stand at this juncture, poised to step into the chapter of **Moving Forward in Faith**, it feels both a continuation and a gentle culmination of the journey we have shared. Together, we have traversed landscapes of the soul, ventured through valleys of surrender, and climbed peaks of trust and grace, discovering along the way that every step, every breath, carries within it a lesson, a blessing, a spark of the divine. Reflecting on our journey so far, It is clear we have embarked on something truly profound. We have explored the depths of surrender, learning to let go of the reins with the trust that the universe has a plan far greater than any we could devise. We have walked the path of grace, finding beauty and lessons in both the light and shadows of our experiences. And through practices steeped in gratitude and presence, we have found a deeper connection to the moment, to ourselves, and to the intricate web of life that surrounds us.

But what makes this journey so special is not just the ground we have covered; It is the companionship we have shared—yours and mine. Through these pages, we have engaged in a silent dialogue, heart to heart, spirit to spirit, reminding each other that we are not alone in our quest for deeper meaning and connection. The road ahead is as much about carrying forward the insights and practices we have gathered as it is about staying open to new lessons, new experiences, new opportunities to grow and deepen our faith. Moving forward in faith is about embracing the unknown with a heart full of courage, a mind open to possibilities, and a spirit willing to dance with the divine mystery that unfolds our path.

I urge you continue your journey with a renewed sense of hope, curiosity, and trust. You can use it as a call to live our lives as a testament to the power of faith, to the resilience of the human spirit, and to the endless grace that guides our way. As we move forward, let us do so with the knowledge that our journey is ever-unfolding, rich with potential for transformation, joy, and deeper connection with the essence of all that is.

Let this not be an end, but a beautiful beginning. A beginning where every moment is an opportunity to practice what we have learned, to share the light we have found, and to extend our hands in kindness and compassion to those we meet along the way. Together, let's step into the next chapter of our journey, moving forward in faith, with hearts wide open to the adventure that awaits.

This new chapter of our journey—moving forward in faith—is not just about applying what we have learned; It is about embodying it. Every interaction, every challenge, every quiet moment becomes a canvas upon which we can paint with the colours of grace, trust, and surrender we have so carefully gathered.

Embracing Life with Openness

Embracing life with an open-heart means welcoming the full spectrum of human experience with acceptance and compassion. It is understanding that joy and sorrow are not opposites but companions on our journey, each offering unique lessons and opportunities for growth. As we move forward, let us cherish the joyful moments with gratitude and approach the challenging ones with the courage to seek out the hidden blessings they contain.

Continuing the Journey of Self-Discovery

The journey inward—a pilgrimage to the core of our being—doesn't end. It deepens. Each day offers a fresh landscape to explore, new facets of our character to uncover, and deeper truths to understand. Moving forward in faith involves a commitment to this ongoing process of self-discovery, to peeling back the layers that obscure our true essence and embracing the luminous being that resides within.

Extending Compassion and Kindness

One of the most beautiful aspects of moving forward in faith is the opportunity to extend the compassion and kindness we have cultivated towards ourselves out into the world. Recognising the interconnectedness of all life, we understand that extending a hand in kindness not only uplifts others but reinforces the web of support and love that sustains us all. Let our interactions be guided by empathy and a genuine desire to contribute to the well-being of others.

Staying Connected to the Source

Maintaining a connection to the divine, or whatever source of guidance and inspiration you resonate with, is crucial as we move forward. Whether through prayer, meditation, nature walks, or creative expression, find ways to nurture this connection. It is from this deep wellspring of spiritual nourishment that we draw the strength, guidance, and peace to navigate life's journey.

Sharing Your Light

As you walk this path, remember that your journey can be a source of inspiration and hope for others. Share your stories, your lessons, and your light. Whether through conversations, writings, art, or simply through the way you live your life, you have the power to be a beacon of faith, grace, and love.

In this journey, each step is a testament to our inner strength and capacity for growth. Imagine a landscape, serene and inviting, where a winding path leads through a lush, vibrant forest toward a radiant horizon. This landscape symbolizes our spiritual journey—a trek through the complexities of life, illuminated by moments of clarity and insight. Along this path, the trees whisper ancient truths, the breeze carries songs of hope, and the ground beneath our feet supports us with unwavering strength. The journey of faith and discovery is akin to navigating this vibrant forest. It is not marked by the miles travelled but by the depth of our experiences and the lessons we absorb along the way. In this serene landscape, we find symbols of our growth, reflections of our resilience, and echoes of our deepest yearnings. Each step forward is a step into ourselves, into the heart of our being, where we discover the sacredness found in the everyday.

Let this image of a journey through a radiant, inviting forest serve as a reminder of our own path of personal and spiritual evolution. It invites us to pause, reflect, and appreciate the beauty of our journey, recognising that spiritual growth unfolds in the tranquillity of our hearts as much as in the challenges we face. In this reflection, we find peace, purpose, and a connection to something greater than ourselves—a link to the divine tapestry that weaves through the fabric of our lives, guiding us toward a horizon filled with light and promise. The serenity and purpose symbolized by this landscape inspire us to embrace our journey with an open heart, to cherish each moment of discovery, and to move with grace through the vibrant forest of life. This journey, rich with potential for enlightenment and transformation, beckons us forward, not with haste, but with the gentle assurance that every step taken in faith is a step towards realising our true essence and the boundless possibilities that await us.

As we emerge from the forest's embrace, stepping into the clearings that grace our path, we carry with us the knowledge that our journey is infinitely enriched by our willingness to embrace it fully. We learn that faith is a companion that walks beside us, a light that guides us through the darkest nights, and a strength that supports us as we climb the steepest paths. We see that surrendering to the journey with an open heart allows us to receive the abundance of gifts it offers, to see the beauty in the challenges, and to find the grace in every step.

Let us then continue to move forward in faith, carrying the lessons of the forest within us. Let us walk with the assurance that every step forward, taken with an open heart and a willing spirit, is a step toward a deeper understanding of ourselves and the divine mystery that envelops us. Let the journey be our teacher, the path our revelation, and faith our guiding star as we navigate the wondrous landscape of life, moving ever onward toward the horizon filled with light and promise, where our true essence and the boundless possibilities of our spirit await discovery.

Thank you for joining me on this journey through "Guided by Grace." I hope you found inspiration and comfort within these pages.

Let's stay connected! Follow me on Instagram **@harsharangillkent** for more insights, inspiration, and updates on my latest projects. I look forward to continuing this journey of growth and discovery together.

With gratitude,
Harsharan Gill-Kent

Printed in Great Britain
by Amazon

42594858R00142